T0290294

Divorce
in Oklahoma

*The Legal Process,
Your Rights, and What to Expect*

Mark Antinoro, Esq.

Addicus Books
Omaha, Nebraska

An Addicus Nonfiction Book

Copyright 2017 by Mark Antinoro. All rights reserved. No part of this publication may be reproduced, stored in a retrieval system, or transmitted in any form or by any means, electronic, mechanical, photocopied, recorded, or otherwise, without the prior written permission of the publisher. For information, write Addicus Books, Inc., P.O. Box 45327, Omaha, Nebraska 68145.

ISBN 978-1-943886-07-4

Typography by Jack Kusler

This book is not intended to serve as a substitute for an attorney. Nor is it the author's intent to give legal advice contrary to that of an attorney.

Library of Congress Cataloging-in-Publication Data
Names: Antinoro, Mark, 1969—author.
Title: Divorce in Oklahoma : the legal process, your rights, and what to expect / Mark Antinoro, Esq.
Description: Omaha, Nebraska : Addicus Books, Inc., [2016] | Includes index.
Identifiers: LCCN 2016034513 (print) | LCCN 2016035176 (e-book) | ISBN 9781943886074 (alk. paper) | ISBN 9781943886555 (PDF) | ISBN 9781943886579 (MOBI) | ISBN 9781943886562 (EPUB)
Subjects: LCSH: Divorce—Law and legislation—Oklahoma. | Separation (Law)—Oklahoma.
Classification: LCC KFO1300 .A95 2016 (print) | LCC KFO1300 (ebook) | DDC 346.76601/66—dc23
LC record available at https://lccn.loc.gov/2016034513

Addicus Books, Inc.
P.O. Box 45327
Omaha, Nebraska 68145
www.AddicusBooks.com
Printed in the United States of America
10 9 8 7 6 5 4 3 2 1

To my mother, Linda Wilson Antinoro.
My mother raised my brother, Scott, and me as
a single mother. She made many sacrifices for
her children and always did so selflessly.
Her tireless drive is the source of my work ethic.
Whatever accomplishments that I may have,
such as they are, would not have been
possible without her encouragement
and devotion to her sons.

Contents

Introduction

For most people, divorce can be one of the most difficult situations they will encounter in their life. Children and money are two of the most important and stressful concerns in most people's lives and most divorces impact both of these subjects. That sets the stage for many potential problems. My hope in writing *Divorce in Oklahoma* is to help you gain insight into the problems and solutions associated with divorce. I hope this book will be used not only by people going through divorce, but also by professionals who support them—attorneys, mediators, therapists, clergy, financial advisors, coaches, and others who are called upon during the divorce process.

The divorce process can be extremely frustrating. It is not easy to devise a visitation schedule for children without making one or both parents upset. And even though you can divide income and assets in half, in many cases this also causes upset in the short term for both spouses.

Please keep in mind throughout the divorce process that you may become very angry or emotional at times. Logic and reason can often be overcome by emotion. This rarely helps your case and, more often than not, things said and done while in an emotional state have negative consequences in the divorce.

At the outset of a divorce, try to determine whether you could benefit from counseling. Individuals who have issues with anger or depression, or very emotional people, may find counseling or therapy helpful during this period. A counselor/

therapist can help you cope during trying times and can also teach you coping tools for when you feel you are overwhelmed. Your attorney or your doctor should be able to provide the names of counselors/therapists who can be immensely valuable to you. A divorce is not a time to go it alone or to try to tough it out in silence.

Every divorce is unique and you may feel like you are the only one in the world who is going through something like this. Know that is not the case and things will get better.

Like anything in life, you cannot control everything that happens in the divorce process, but you do have absolute control and power over how you react to things. So if your soon-to-be ex-spouse is a half hour late for picking up the children at the exchange point, it can be extremely upsetting but try to keep it in perspective. Don't start out subscribing ill will. Perhaps traffic was extra heavy. Having the right mental attitude throughout the divorce process can make a huge difference in your ability to cope with events.

1

Understanding the Divorce Process

At a time when your life can feel like it's in utter chaos, sometimes the smallest bit of predictability can bring a sense of comfort. The outcome of many aspects of your divorce may be unknown, driving up your fear and anxiety. Develop a basic understanding of the divorce process. This will lower your anxiety when your attorney starts talking about "depositions" or "going to trial" and you feel your heart start pounding in fear. Understanding the divorce process can reduce your frustration about the length of the process because you understand why each step is needed. Most importantly, understanding the divorce process will make your experience of the entire divorce easier. Who wouldn't prefer that?

1.1   Must I have an attorney to get a divorce in Oklahoma?

You are not required to have an attorney to obtain a divorce in Oklahoma. However, if your case involves children, alimony, significant property, or debts I would strongly urge you to hire an attorney.

If your divorce doesn't involve any of the items listed above, there are kits that you can buy on the Internet to complete a divorce, but be advised that these kits have limitations and the author is not recommending them. Of the three law schools in Oklahoma, two have legal clinics that may provide some aid in a divorce: the University of Oklahoma law school and the Oklahoma City University School of Law. Legal Aid of Oklahoma is a nonprofit organization that will help women in divorces if there are issues of domestic violence, but otherwise they are not available for divorce assistance.

If you are considering proceeding without an attorney, at a minimum have an initial consultation with an attorney to discuss your rights and duties under the law. You may have certain rights or obligations about which you are unaware. Meeting with a lawyer can help you decide whether to proceed on your own.

1.2   What is my first step?

Find a law firm that handles divorces as a regular part of its law practice. The best recommendations come from people who have knowledge of a lawyer's experience and reputation.

Even if you are not ready to file for divorce, call to schedule an appointment right away to obtain information about protecting yourself and your children. Even if you are not planning to file for divorce, your spouse might be.

Ask what documents you should bring to your initial consultation. Make a list of your questions to bring to your first meeting. Start making plans for how you will pay your attorney to begin work on your case.

1.3   Is Oklahoma a *no-fault state* or do I need grounds for a divorce?

Oklahoma, like most states, is a *no-fault divorce state*. This means that neither you nor your spouse is required to prove that the other is "at fault" in order to be granted a divorce. Oklahoma provides twelve separate grounds for divorce, which include adultery, extreme cruelty, or abandonment. Alleging these grounds and actually being awarded a divorce based on these grounds is quite rare. However, it may benefit you to request a divorce based upon one of these specific grounds. Discuss this possibility with your lawyer. Keep in mind, a divorce and the documents associated with it are matters of public record. Although you might be very angry with your spouse right now, consider the long-term implications. For example, your small children may one day read that you requested the divorce because your spouse cheated on you.

The overwhelming number of divorces in Oklahoma are granted on grounds of *irreconcilable incompatibility*. In other words, you cannot get along. The court for the most part is not interested in why you are divorcing unless, for example, the reason may have some impact on the children.

The testimony by you or your spouse is likely to be sufficient evidence for the court to rule that the marriage should be dissolved. This testimony, usually given by the spouse who filed for the divorce, will state that efforts at reconciliation were made, that those efforts were not successful, that further attempts would not be beneficial, and that the marriage is irretrievably broken.

1.4   Do I have to get divorced in the same state I married in?

No. Regardless of where you were married, you may seek a divorce in Oklahoma if the jurisdictional requirements of residency are met.

1.5   How long do I have to have lived in Oklahoma to get a divorce in the state?

Either you or your spouse must have been a resident of Oklahoma for at least six months to meet the residency requirement for a divorce in Oklahoma. If neither party meets the residency requirement, other legal options are available for your protection. If you do not meet the residency requirement, talk to your attorney about options such as a legal separation, a petition for a custody and support order, or a protection order.

1.6   My spouse has told me she will never "give me" a divorce. Can I get one in Oklahoma anyway?

Yes. Oklahoma does not require that your spouse "agree to" a divorce. If your spouse threatens to "not give you a divorce," know that in Oklahoma this will not stop the divorce from going forward.

Under Oklahoma law, to obtain a divorce you must be able to prove that what exists between the two of you is irreconcilable incompatibility. Evidence of this will be your testimony on the witness stand.

The Divorce Process

The divorce process in Oklahoma typically involves the following steps.

If you are initiating the divorce:

- Obtain a referral for a lawyer.
- Schedule an appointment with an attorney.
- Prepare questions and gather necessary documents for an initial consultation.
- Meet for an initial consultation with an attorney.
- Pay the attorney a retainer and sign a retainer agreement.
- Provide requested information and documents to your attorney.
- Take other actions as advised by your attorney, such as opening or closing financial accounts.
- Attorney prepares the summons and notice of automatic temporary injunction and petition for dissolution for your review and signature.
- Attorney files the summons and petition with the clerk of the court.
- Attorney has process server serve summons and petition on the respondent.
- If you need more immediate help in areas such as temporary child support, spousal support, or attorney fees, your attorney prepares an application for temporary orders for your review and signature, files with the court, obtains court date, and serves pleadings on respondent.

If you have been served with divorce papers:

- Obtain a referral for a lawyer.
- Schedule an appointment with an attorney.
- Prepare questions and gather necessary documents for an initial consultation.
- Meet for an initial consultation with an attorney.
- Pay the attorney a retainer and sign a retainer agreement.

- Provide requested information and documents to your attorney.
- Take other actions as advised by your attorney.
- Attorney prepares a response to the summons and petition for your review and signature.
- Attorney files your response and counterclaim with the clerk of the court within twenty days of service of the petition and summons on you.
- You may file your own application for temporary orders.
- If you are served with requests for a temporary order, attorney prepares your response to these papers.

After the divorce process has been started and the response has been filed:

- One or both of the attorneys often will send out discovery, questions and requests for certain documents that you and your attorney will work on producing.
- Negotiations begin regarding temporary custody and visitation, child and spousal support, payment of debts, and attorney fees.
- If there are minor children, both parties are required prior to the divorce being finalized to attend a Parents Helping Children Cope with Divorce Seminar and in some counties you may also have to attend a presentation by a judge who urges you and your spouse to get along for the sake of your children.
- Court holds hearing(s) on requests for temporary relief.
- Either the parties reach an agreement or the court issues temporary orders.
- Temporary order is prepared by one attorney, approved as to form by the other attorney, and submitted to the judge for signature.
- If discovery has not been sent out, it likely will be, with both sides sending their questions to the other and possibly sending subpoenas to people or companies

who are not part of the divorce to obtain additional information.

- You confer with your attorney to review facts, identify issues, assess strengths and weaknesses the of case, review strategy, and develop a settlement proposal.
- Spouses, with the support of their attorneys, attempt to reach agreement through written proposals, mediation, settlement conferences, or other forms of negotiation.

If you reach an agreement on all issues, then:

- One attorney prepares marital settlement agreement and necessary judgment paperwork.
- Both parties and their attorneys sign agreement and all necessary paperwork.
- Judgment paperwork is filed with the court.
- Either the parties waive the court date or the court holds a brief, final hearing.
- A decree of dissolution of marriage is entered and you will be divorced.
- Your attorney completes necessary orders and supervises the property transfer until all agreed terms are satisfied.

If you are unable to reach an agreement on all issues, then:

- Your attorney completes all necessary discovery in order to bring the case to its trial-ready point.
- Your attorney files a request to have an application for a pretrial conference and typically the attorneys speak to the judge about the merits of the case and a trial date is usually given. (Some judges will order you to attend mediation sessions at this point before giving you a trial date.)
- If agreement has been reached on any issues, your attorney prepares a stipulation on those issues. All other issues are set for trial.
- You work with your attorney to prepare your case for trial.

- Your attorney prepares witnesses, trial exhibits, legal research on contested issues, pretrial motions, trial briefs, direct and cross-examination of witnesses, opening statements, witness subpoenas, and your closing argument.
- You meet with your attorney for final trial preparation.
- Trial is held.
- Some judges will issue a decision at that time, but in many cases the judge will take the matter under advisement. Typically, a judge will render his or her written decision that he sends to the parties' attorney within two weeks. However, by statute a judge is required to render a decision within sixty days of taking a matter under advisement.
- After the judge renders his or her decision, it is more formally written up by one of the attorneys, typically the attorney for the *petitioner* (the party who filed for divorce). The decree of dissolution must be signed by both attorneys.
- If the attorneys cannot agree on certain areas where the judge was not clear or if there is a disagreement, a motion to settle is filed and another court date is held where the judge resolves the areas that are in dispute.
- The judge signs the decree of dissolution of marriage.

Your posttrial rights are discussed in chapter 16.

1.7 Can I divorce my spouse in Oklahoma if he or she lives in another state?

Provided you have met the residency requirements for living in Oklahoma for six months, you can file for divorce here even if your spouse lives in another state. If both of you have lived in more than one state in the last six months and you have children, an issue can arise that involves the *Uniform Child Custody Jurisdiction Enforcement Act (UCCJEA)*. This is a national compact that most of the states have entered into, and you will need to discuss the UCCJEA with your attorney because it can be fairly complex.

1.8   How can I divorce my spouse when I don't know where this person lives now?

Oklahoma law allows you to proceed with a divorce even if you do not know the current address of your spouse. First, take action to attempt to locate your spouse. Contact family members, friends, former coworkers, or anyone else who might know your spouse's whereabouts. Utilize resources on the Internet that are designed to help locate people.

Let your attorney know of the efforts you have made to attempt to find your spouse. Inform your lawyer of your spouse's last known address, as well as any work address or other address where this person may be found. Once your attorney attempts to give notice to your spouse without success, it is possible to ask the court to proceed with the divorce by giving notice through publication in a newspaper.

Although your divorce may be granted following service of notice by publication in a newspaper, you may not be able to get other court orders, such as those for child support or alimony, without giving personal notice to your spouse. As a matter of caution, understand that a divorce that is finalized without ever formally serving your spouse with divorce papers is called a *default divorce* and it is subject to being *vacated* (undone) at a later point. If, for example, your spouse could show that you knew or should have known where to find him at the time the divorce was granted, the divorce could later be vacated. Talk to your lawyer about this issue.

1.9   I just moved to a different county. Do I have to file in the county where my spouse lives?

You may file your divorce petition either in the county where you reside or the county where your spouse resides. However, if a dispute develops over which county has jurisdiction it is likely the county where you and your spouse lived together will be the county for the divorce. If you have children the court will likely look to which county the children have had the most contacts within the last six months.

1.10   I immigrated to Oklahoma. Will my immigration status stop me from getting a divorce?

If you meet the residency requirements for divorce in Oklahoma, you can get a divorce here regardless of your immigration status. Talk to your immigration lawyer about the likelihood of a divorce leading to immigration challenges. If you are a victim of domestic violence, tell your lawyer. You may be eligible for a change in your immigration status under the federal *Violence Against Women Act.*

1.11   I want to get divorced in my Indian tribal court. What do I need to know?

At this time, Oklahoma does not recognize tribal divorces, so you will still need to go through the divorce process at your local county courthouse.

1.12   Is there a waiting period for a divorce in Oklahoma?

Yes. Oklahoma has a mandatory ninety-day waiting period if you have minor children. The ninety-day period can be waived if both parties agree and the judge also agrees. If the parties do not have minor children and they agree to the divorce there is a ten-day waiting period. You cannot remarry for six months.

1.13   What is a *divorce petition*?

A *divorce petition,* also referred to as a *pleading,* is a legal document signed by the person filing for divorce and filed with the clerk of the court to initiate the divorce process. A petition will explain in very general terms what the plaintiff is asking the court to order. See the Sample Petition in the Appendix.

1.14   My spouse said she filed for divorce last week, but my lawyer says there's nothing on file at the courthouse. What does it mean to "file for divorce"?

When lawyers use the term "filing" they are usually referring to the physical act of taking legal documents to the courthouse, such as the petition for divorce. It is handed to the clerk of the court and the clerk affixes their stamp on it, proving that it has been filed. Sometimes a person who has hired a lawyer to begin a divorce action uses the phrase, "I've filed for divorce," although no actual papers have yet been taken to the courthouse to start the legal process. Until the filing fee has been paid and the clerk puts his or her stamp on the petition you haven't actually "filed."

1.15   If we both want a divorce, does in matter who files?

There is a common misperception that by filing first you gain some advantage. Unless you are requesting some type of emergency relief or a victim protective order (which will be discussed later), there is no advantage to filing first. In fact, by filing first you would pay the filing fee, which is approximately $210 and the service of process fee of usually $60 to $75.

In years past, in Oklahoma, the person who filed the divorce first was called the *plaintiff* and the other party was referred to as the *defendant*. Because many people believed that if they were called the "defendant" they were at a disadvantage, the Oklahoma legislature changed the names of the parties to *petitioner* (person who files first) and *respondent* (person who responds to the divorce petition).

1.16   Can I stop the newspaper from publishing notice of the filing or granting of my divorce?

No. Documents filed with the court, such as a divorce petition, are a matter of public record. Newspapers have a right to access this information, and many newspapers publish this information as a matter of routine. Newspapers that publish such notices typically do so within a week of the date that documents are filed with the court clerk.

In very rare cases, portions of a divorce file may be kept private. These cases are referred to as being "sealed" or "under seal." It is not easy to get this exception and you should not expect your lawyer to accomplish this.

1.17   Is there a way to avoid embarrassing my spouse and not have the sheriff serve him with the divorce papers at his workplace?

Talk to your lawyer about the option of having your spouse sign a document known as a *waiver*. The signing and filing of a waiver with the court can eliminate the need to have your spouse served by a process server. See the Sample Letter to Spouse on the following page.

Sample Letter to Spouse

 ANTINORO LAW FIRM, PLC
Mark Antinoro
Attorney-at-Law
25 North Vann Street
Pryor, OK 74362

John Smith
1234 First Street
City, OK 74967

RE: Smith v. Smith

Dear Mr. Smith:

This office has been retained by Mrs. Smith to represent her in the above entitled divorce matter. Enclosed is a copy of the Petition for Dissolution of Marriage and the Summons and Automatic Temporary Injunction, as well as entry of appearance and waiver of service.

By signing and returning the Voluntary Appearance to my office at the above address you are avoiding the need to have a process server serve you with the above stated documents at your home or place of employment.

Kindly return the Voluntary Appearance to my office in the enclosed envelope no later than December 9, 20__. If I do not receive same by that date, I will assume you have no intention of signing it and I will have you served.

If you have retained an attorney, please ask him or her to contact my office. It is our desire to resolve this matter as amicably as possible for the benefit of you and Mrs. Smith.

Thank you for your cooperation in this matter.

Best regards,

Mark Antinoro, Esq.
Enclosures
cc: Mrs. Smith

1.18 Should I sign an *entry of appearance and voluntary waiver of service* even if I don't agree with what my spouse has written in the petition for divorce?

Signing the *entry of appearance and waiver of service* does not mean that you agree with anything your spouse has stated or anything that your spouse is asking for in the divorce. Signing this form only substitutes for having the process server personally hand you the documents. You do not waive the right to object to anything your spouse has stated in the petition for divorce. Note: Just make sure you are only signing a waiver of service and not waiving the right to file a response or to contest the divorce.

1.19 If I have received divorce papers, why should I contact an attorney right away?

If your spouse has filed for divorce, it is important that you obtain legal advice as soon as possible. Even if you and your spouse are getting along, having independent legal counsel can help you make decisions now that could affect your divorce later. Keep in mind that throughout the divorce process, preparation is critical and the more time you and your attorney have to prepare, the better off you will be.

Attorneys tend to have their schedules filled fairly far in advance, so the sooner you call the attorney's office, the sooner you will get an appointment. After your spouse has filed for divorce, a temporary hearing is often scheduled within three to four weeks and sometimes it may be set as short as two weeks.

1.20 What is a *temporary hearing?*

A *temporary hearing* is a court proceeding, usually at the beginning of the divorce case, in which the judge decides what arrangements will be made with the divorcing couple until their case is completed. This hearing can determine such things as temporary custody or visitation schedule, temporary spousal support, child-support payments, preventing the parties from using marital assets, or any other temporary issue while you await trial. You will be better prepared for a temporary hearing if you have already retained an attorney.

1.21 What is an *ex parte/emergency court order?*

An *ex parte court order* is obtained by only one party going to the judge to ask for some type of relief. This often involves allegations of some type of emergency situation, such as a spouse using drugs. Often called emergency orders, most *ex parte* requests involve protection of children.

Ordinarily the court will require the other party to have notice of any requests for court orders, and a hearing before the judge will be helpful, so *ex parte* requests are an exception to the rule. A *protective order (victim protective order)* is technically a separate cause of action, but in many cases it gets consolidated into the divorce and is very common in a contested divorce. See chapter 7 for more information on emergency situations.

An *affidavit,* which is a written statement sworn under oath, is usually required before a judge will sign an *ex parte* order. Some judges will require testimony by the spouse requesting the relief. When an *ex parte* order is granted, the party who did not request the order will have an opportunity to have a subsequent hearing before the judge to determine whether the order should remain in effect. Typically, this is done within ten days. This hearing is called a *show-cause hearing.*

A word of caution on *ex parte*/emergency orders in general: When one spouse becomes upset with the other spouse, especially as it relates to the children, emotions can run very high. Often, at an emergency *ex parte* hearing there is a tendency for a spouse to exaggerate allegations that cannot be supported by any objective evidence. There will be a show-cause hearing, where the other spouse's attorney can challenge the allegations. If the spouse who made the allegations cannot substantiate them, not only will the *ex parte* order be dismissed, but it can have a lasting impact on that spouse's credibility with the judge throughout the divorce process. If your attorney suggests that your situation may not rise to the level of an emergency in the judge's eyes, please listen to your attorney.

1.22 What is a *motion?*

A *motion* is a request that the judge enter a court order to grant you something or to stop your spouse from doing something. For example, your attorney may file a written motion requesting that your spouse be ordered to take a drug test.

1.23 Once my petition for divorce is filed, how long will it take before a temporary hearing is held to decide what happens with our child and our finances while the divorce is pending?

A temporary hearing will be set typically within three to four weeks of your divorce being filed with the court, assuming your spouse can be located to be given notice. There is a difference between the hearing being scheduled and getting an actual hearing date. Depending on your particular county, some judges are merely setting the matter on a docket with other cases, which enables the attorneys and judge to talk to one another, but no testimony is taken. Some counties may give you an actual hearing date. Your attorney will tell you which practice your county follows.

1.24 How much notice will I get if my spouse seeks a temporary order?

Most judges will grant a *continuance* (a new court date) if you were served with divorce papers in ten days or less.

1.25 During my divorce, what am I responsible for doing?

Your attorney will explain what actions you should take to further the divorce process and to help you reach the best possible outcome.

You will be asked to:

- Keep in regular contact with your attorney.
- Update your attorney regarding any changes in your contact information, such as address, phone numbers, and e-mail address.
- Provide your attorney with all requested documents.
- Provide requested information in a timely manner.
- Complete forms and questionnaires.
- Appear in court on time.
- Be direct about asking any questions you might have.
- Tell your attorney your thoughts on settlement or what you would like the judge to order in your case.

- Remain respectful toward your spouse throughout the process.
- Comply with any temporary court orders, such as restraining or support orders.
- Advise your attorney of any significant developments in your case.

By doing your part in the divorce process, you enable your attorney to partner with you for a better outcome while also lowering your attorney fees.

1.26 I'm worried that I won't remember to ask my lawyer about all of the issues in my case. How can I be sure I don't miss anything?

Write down all of the topics you want to discuss with your attorney, including what your goals are for the outcome of the divorce. A Divorce Issues Checklist (see sample) can be a useful tool. The sooner you get clear about your goals, the easier it will be for your attorney to support you to get what you want. Realize that your attorney will likely think of some issues that you may not have considered.

Divorce Issues Checklist

Issue	Notes
Dissolution of marriage—divorce	
Custody of minor children	
Removal of children from jurisdiction	
Visitation (time share) plan (time, transportation)	
Child support	
Monitor your spouse's social media sites	
Summer child-support abatement	
Life insurance to fund unpaid child support	
Automatic withholding for support	
Child-care expenses	
Health insurance on minor children	

Divorce Issues Checklist (Continued)

Issue	Notes
Uninsured medical expenses for minor children	
Private school tuition for children	
Child's special needs	
Health insurance on the parties of children	
Real property: marital residence (deed, refinancing, sale)	
Real property: rentals, cabins, commercial property (deed, refinancing, sale)	
Marital expenses associated with real estate	
Time-shares (real estate)	
Retirement plans (401k, Simple IRA, TSA) possible federal or military pensions	
Businesses	
Bank accounts	
Investments	
Stock options	
Premarital or nonmarital assets	
Premarital or nonmarital debts	
Pets	
Personal property division: including motor vehicles, recreational vehicles, campers, airplanes, collections, furniture, electronics, tools, household goods	
Exchange date for personal property	
Division of marital debt	
Property settlement	
Alimony	
Life insurance to fund unpaid alimony	
Sums owed under temporary order	

Divorce Issues Checklist (Continued)

Issue	Notes
Tax exemptions for minor children	
IRS Form 8332 for claiming children as dependents	
Filing status for tax returns for last/current year	
Restoration of former name	
Attorney fees	

1.27 My spouse has all of our financial information. How will I be able to prepare for negotiations and trial if I don't know the facts or have the documents?

After your divorce has been filed with the court and temporary matters have been addressed, your attorney will proceed with a process known as *discovery*. Through discovery, your attorney can ask your spouse or even third parties, such as banks, to provide documents and information needed to prepare your case. The more information that you can provide your attorney, the better he or she can tailor certain requests. The discovery process is covered in more detail in chapter 5.

1.28 My spouse and I both want our divorce to be amicable. How can we keep it that way?

This is going to be possible only if you are both reasonable and cooperate with each other. Cooperation will not only make your lives easier and save you money on attorney fees, but it is also more likely to result in an outcome you are both satisfied with.

Find a lawyer who understands your goal to reach settlement and encourage your spouse to do the same. Then ask your attorney about the options of mediation and negotiation for reaching agreement. (See chapter 6 for a discussion of mediation and negotiation.) Even if you are not able to settle all of the issues in your divorce, you can narrow down the issues, which will reduce stress and costs.

1.29 Can I get a different judge?

You cannot get another judge simply because you did not like the way the judge ruled in the temporary order hearing. You must have specific and personal reasons why you believe the judge cannot be fair. If you believe that your judge has a *conflict of interest,* such as being a close friend with your spouse's father, you may have a basis for asking the judge to be *recused* (to withdraw from the case) in order to allow another judge to hear the case. This is not easy to do, and most judges will oppose it, viewing it as an attack on their character. Talk to your attorney about the reasons you want a different judge.

1.30 How long will it take to get my divorce?

The more you and your spouse are in agreement, the faster your divorce will conclude. At a minimum, there will be a ninety-day wait from the date of the service of the divorce petition if you have children. However, a judge can waive this period if both parties request it and the divorce appears to be an amicable one. A hotly contested divorce can last many years, but fortunately this is the exception and not the rule.

1.31 What is the significance of my divorce being final?

The finality of your divorce decree, sometimes referred to as the *decree of dissolution of marriage,* is important for many reasons. It can affect your right to remarry, your eligibility for health insurance from your former spouse, and your filing status for income taxes.

1.32 When does my divorce become final?

The date that triggers the time period for a divorce becoming final is the date that the divorce decree is filed with the court clerk. In most cases, this will be the day the judge signs your divorce decree or the next business day. On rare occasions, the day the judge signs the decree is not the day that it gets filed. This can occur, for example, if the judge signs the decree at the end of the day and it does not go immediately to the clerk of the court.

For most purposes, your divorce is final thirty days from the date it is entered by the court. You may not remarry until six months after the decree was filed.

1.33 Can I start using my former name right away and how do I get my name legally restored?

You may begin using your former name at any time, provided you are not doing so for any unlawful purpose, such as to avoid your creditors. Note that many agencies and institutions will not alter their records without a court order showing a change in your name. After the decree has been finalized, one of your first acts should be taking a certified copy of the decree to your nearest Social Security office to update their records.

If you want your former name restored, let your attorney know so that this provision can be included in your divorce decree. Your spouse cannot require you to change your name; nor can he stop you from changing your name. If you want to change your legal name after the divorce and have not provided for it in your decree, it will be necessary for you to undergo an entirely separate court action with filing fees.

2

Coping with Stress
during the Divorce Process

It may have been a few years ago, or it may have been many years ago. Perhaps it was only months. But, when you said, "I do," you meant it. Like most people getting married, you planned to be a happily married couple for life.

But things happen. Life brings change. People change. Whatever the circumstance, you now find yourself considering divorce. The emotions of divorce run from one extreme to another as you journey through the process. You may feel relief and ready to move on with your life. On the other hand, you may feel emotions that are quite painful. Anger. Fear. Sorrow. A deep sense of loss or failure. It is important to find support for coping with all these strong emotions.

Because going through a divorce can be an emotional time, having a clear understanding of the divorce process and what to expect will help you make better decisions. And, when it comes to decision making, search inside yourself to clarify your intentions and goals for the future. Let these intentions be your guide.

2.1   My spouse left home weeks ago. I don't want a divorce because I feel our marriage can be saved. Should I still see an attorney?

It's a good idea to see an attorney. Whether you want a divorce or not, there may be important actions for you to take now to protect your assets, credit, home, children, and future right to support.

If your spouse files for divorce, a temporary hearing could be heard in just a matter of days. It is best to be prepared with the support of an attorney, even if you decide not to file for a divorce at this time.

2.2   The thought of going to a lawyer's office to talk about divorce is more than I can bear. I canceled the first appointment I made because I just couldn't do it. What should I do?

Many people going through a divorce are dealing with lawyers for the first time and feel anxious about the experience. Ask a trusted friend or family member to go with you. He or she can support you by writing down your questions in advance, by taking notes for you during the meeting, and by helping you to remember what the lawyer said after the meeting is concluded. It is very likely that you will feel greatly relieved just to be better informed.

2.3   There is some information about my marriage that I think my attorney needs, but I'm too embarrassed to discuss it. Must I tell the attorney?

Your attorney has an ethical duty to maintain confidentiality. Past events in your marriage are matters that your lawyer is obligated to keep private.

Attorneys who practice divorce law are accustomed to hearing a lot of intimate information about families. While it is deeply personal to you, it is unlikely that anything you tell your lawyer will be a shock. In most cases your spouse will be sharing similar information with her or his attorney. You don't want to have your attorney be surprised during a hearing by information that you should have shared with him or her at the outset.

I cannot tell you how many times after a hearing I have had the client say, "I didn't tell you about that because I didn't think she would bring that up; it was so long ago." Hoping that something will not be brought up is not a good idea. Let your attorney decide what is and what is not important. If speaking directly about these facts still seems too hard, consider putting them in a letter or e-mail to your attorney.

2.4 I'm unsure about how to tell our children about the divorce, and I'm worried I'll say the wrong thing. What's the best way?

How you talk to your children about the divorce will depend upon their ages and development. Changes in your children's everyday lives, such as a change of residence or one parent leaving the home, are far more important to them. Information about legal proceedings and meetings with lawyers is best kept among adults.

Simpler answers are best for young children. Avoid giving them more information than they need. Seek out your counselor or friends as a source of support to meet your own emotional needs. Regardless of your children's ages, you must refrain from speaking ill of your spouse in front of the children. By not speaking poorly of your spouse, you are helping your children cope with what can be an extremely upsetting process for them. I know this is easier said than done, but always keep the future in mind—the divorce process will eventually come to a close.

After the initial discussion, keep the door open by creating opportunities for your children to talk about the divorce. Use these times to acknowledge their feelings and offer support. Always assure them that the divorce is not their fault and that they are still loved by both you and your spouse.

2.5 My youngest child seems very depressed about the divorce, the middle one is angry, and my teenager is skipping school. How can I help them?

A child's reaction to divorce can vary depending upon his or her age and other factors. Some may cry and beg for a reconciliation, and others may act out. Reducing conflict with your spouse, being a consistent and nurturing parent, and making sure both of you remain involved with the children are all actions that can support your children regardless of how they are reacting to the divorce.

A school counselor can provide support; make the teachers aware of your situation. If more help is needed, confer with a therapist experienced in working with children.

2.6   I am so frustrated by my spouse's "Disneyland parent" behavior. Is there anything I can do to stop this?

Feelings of guilt, competition, or remorse may tempt a parent to spend parenting time on special activities.

This can be very frustrating if you are the parent who enforces the rules. Try to work with your spouse to establish consistent discipline and routines for the children. Realize, though, that the other spouse will not always agree.

It is fairly common for some children and teenagers to express a preference for the parent whose disciplining style is the least restrictive. Make sure when either you or your attorney has an opportunity to address the judge that you make it clear that you don't think you should be penalized for being the parent who holds the child accountable for their actions. Most judges value appropriate disciplining and view it positively.

Do your best to be an outstanding parent during this time. This includes keeping a routine for your child for meals, bedtimes, chores, and homework. Encourage family activities as well as individual time with each child when it's possible. During a time when your child's life is changing, providing a stable home life can ease their anxiety and provide comfort.

2.7   Between requests for information from my spouse's lawyer and my own lawyer, I am totally overwhelmed. How do I manage to gather all of this detailed information by the deadlines imposed?

These requests for information can be a taxing process, but don't ignore them and pretend they will go away. Do not put off this task. You must get started as soon as possible. Delays can create problems. Depending on the extent of the delay, it may provide a reason for your spouse's attorney to request that you pay his or her fees. See question 5.4 in chapter 5 for a more detailed discussion about the importance of supplying information promptly.

2.8   I am so depressed about my divorce that I'm having difficulty getting out of bed in the morning to care for my children. What should I do?

See your health care provider and follow their advice. Feelings of depression are common during a divorce. You also want to make sure that you identify any physical health concerns.

Although feelings of sadness are common during a divorce, more serious depression means it's time to seek professional support. If you have to use your children as a motivational tool to get you going, do it.

Keep in mind that this process is going to lead to a new chapter in your life. Think of it as an opportunity for a fresh start. You can do this!

2.9   I know I need help to cope with the stress of the divorce, but I can't afford counseling. What can I do?

You are wise to recognize that divorce is a time for seeking support. You can explore a number of options, including:

- Meeting with a member of the clergy or lay chaplain
- Joining a divorce support group
- Turning to friends and family members
- Finding out if the Oklahoma Department of Human Services (see Resources for contact information) may be able to refer you to counselors who offer free services or operate on a sliding-fee scale.

If none of these options are available, look again at your budget. You may see that counseling is important enough that you can find a way to increase your income or lower your expenses to support this investment in your well-being. Some insurance policies cover mental health care.

2.10   I'm the one who filed for divorce, but I still have loving feelings for my spouse and feel sad about divorcing. Does this mean I should dismiss my divorce?

Whether or not to proceed with a divorce is a deeply personal decision. Strong feelings of caring about your spouse often persist after a divorce is filed. While feelings can inform us of our thoughts, sometimes they can also cause us to not look at everything there is to see in our situation.

Have you and your spouse participated in marriage counseling? Has your spouse refused to seek treatment for an addiction? Are you worried about the safety of you or your children if you remain in the marriage? Is your spouse involved in another relationship?

The answers to these questions can help you get clear about whether to consider reconciliation. Talk to your therapist, counselor, or spiritual advisor to help determine the right path for you.

2.11 Will my lawyer charge me for the time I spend talking about my feelings about my spouse and my divorce?

Yes. Lawyers charge an hourly rate for their time regardless of what aspect of your case is being discussed.

2.12 My lawyer doesn't seem to realize how difficult my divorce is for me. How can I get him to understand?

You may need to seek more support from a friend or a therapist rather than empathy from your lawyer. Divorce lawyers understand the process is very trying, but realistically they cannot always assuage your feelings of anguish and fear.

2.13 I've been told not to speak ill of my spouse in front of my child, but I know my spouse is doing this all the time. Why can't I just speak the truth?

It can be devastating for your child to hear you bad-mouthing his mother or father. What your child needs is permission to love both of you, regardless of any bad parental behavior. The best way to support your child during this time is to encourage a positive relationship with the other parent. Your lawyer can ask the judge to admonish both sides not to speak ill of the other party in front of the children. This instruction may be written into a temporary order.

2.14 Nobody in our family has ever been divorced and I feel really ashamed. Will my children feel the same way?

It has been estimated that 50 percent of marriages end in divorce. So you are by no means alone. You can be a great teacher to them during this time by demonstrating pride in your family and in yourself. Your children will have an opportunity to witness you overcoming obstacles, demonstrating independence, and moving forward in your life.

2.15 I am terrified of having my *deposition* taken. My spouse's lawyer is very aggressive, and I'm afraid I'm going to say something that will hurt my case. What can I do?

A *deposition* is a formal proceeding in which the other party's lawyer will ask you questions under oath and a court reporter will take down your answers. A deposition is an opportunity for your spouse's attorney to gather information and to assess the type of witness you will be if the case proceeds to trial. Feeling anxious about your deposition is normal.

Generally speaking, a lawyer has much greater latitude in the type of questions that they can inquire about during a deposition than in an actual trial. Because a topic was asked about in a deposition doesn't mean that the lawyer will be able to ask you about it again during a trial.

The other party's lawyer may want to see if she or he can rattle you. If you are a person who is easily upset, role-play and have your lawyer find someone else to ask you mock questions prior to your deposition. At a minimum you will want to meet with your lawyer before the deposition to prepare. Ask your lawyer what areas she or he thinks might come up that might be challenging for you. Remember that your attorney will be seated by your side at all times to support you. See questions 5.7 to 5.17 in chapter 5 for a more extensive discussion of depositions.

2.16 I am still so angry at my spouse. How can I be expected to sit in the same room during a mediation?

If you are still really angry at your spouse, it may be beneficial to postpone the conference for a time. You might also consider seeking counseling if you haven't done this already. Counseling can help support you in coping with your feelings of anger.

Be aware that most mediations are conducted with the spouses and their attorneys in separate rooms. Settlement offers are then relayed between the attorneys throughout the negotiation process. But this arrangement doesn't always help. In addition to being a family law attorney, I also am a certified mediator and in many instances keeping the husband and wife in separate rooms makes it much harder to reach an agreement.

You may know people who are much more impolite in e-mail than they are in person. This is often what happens when spouses are in separate rooms during divorce mediation.

2.17 I'm afraid I can't make it through court without having an emotional breakdown. How do I prepare?

A divorce trial can be a highly emotional time, calling for lots of support. Some of these ideas may help you get through the process more easily:

- Meet with your lawyer or the firm's support staff in advance of your court date to prepare you for court.
- Ask your lawyer whether there are any documents you should review in preparation for court, such as your deposition.
- Visit the courtroom in advance to get comfortable with the surroundings.
- Ask your lawyer about having a support person with you on your court date.
- Ask yourself what the worst thing is that could happen and consider what options you would have if it did.
- Discuss with your doctor before taking prescription drugs like valium as they may calm you down but may also negatively impact your overall testimony.
- Visualize the experience going well. Picture yourself sitting in the witness stand, giving clear, confident, and truthful answers to easy questions.
- Arrive early at the courthouse. Cutting it too close in time will only cause additional stress.
- Take slow, deep breaths. Breathing deeply will steady your voice, calm your nerves, and improve your focus.

Your attorney will be prepared to support you throughout the proceedings.

2.18 I am really confused. One day I think I've made a mistake, the next day I know I can't go back, and a few minutes later I can hardly wait to be single again. Some days I just don't believe I'm getting divorced. What's happening?

What you are experiencing is normal for a person going through divorce. Denial, transition, and acceptance are common passages during the divorce process. One moment you might feel excited about your future, and a few hours later you may think your life is ruined.

What can be helpful to remember is that you may not pass from one stage to the next in a direct line. Feelings of anger or sadness may well up in you long after you thought you had moved on. Similarly, your mood might feel bright as you think about your future plans, even though you still miss your spouse.

3

Working with an Attorney

Your lawyer should be someone whom you can trust and who will advise you through this arduous process. Your attorney should also be able to tell you when she or he thinks you are being unreasonable or are about to make a mistake. The counsel of your attorney can impact your life for years to come. An attorney may have to calculate factors into your case that may not be obvious to you, so you want to select an attorney who communicates well with you. You will never regret taking the time and energy to choose the right one for you.

3.1 Where do I begin looking for an attorney for my divorce?

One good source to check is Martindale-Hubbell—an information service for the legal profession since 1868. This directory will tell you about the types of law in which attorneys practice. See www.martindale.com.

This directory is also the most respected source for rating attorneys in all fifty states. The highest rating a lawyer can attain is an AV rating, but there are plenty of good lawyers who are BV rated. Ask people you trust—friends and family members—who have gone through divorce, if they thought they had a great lawyer (or if their former spouse did!). If you know professionals who work with attorneys, ask for a referral to an attorney who is experienced in family law.

When going online to look for an attorney be careful not to judge the attorney by the website design. There are plenty of outstanding attorneys who have very modest websites, and likewise there are plenty of inexperienced attorneys who have fancy websites.

3.2   How do I choose the right attorney?

Choosing the right attorney for your divorce is an important decision. Your attorney should be a trusted professional with whom you feel comfortable sharing information openly. You will rely upon your attorney to help you make many decisions throughout the course of your divorce. You will also entrust your legal counsel to make a range of strategic and procedural decisions on your behalf.

Consultation for a divorce might be your first meeting with a lawyer. Know that attorneys want to be supportive and to fully inform you. Feel free to seek all of the information you need to help you feel secure in knowing you have made the right choice.

Find an attorney who practices primarily in the family law area. Determine the level of experience you want in your attorney. For example, if you have a short marriage with no children and few assets, an attorney with lesser experience might be a good value for your legal needs. However, if you are anticipating a custody dispute or have complex or substantial assets, a more experienced attorney may better meet your needs.

Consider the qualities in an attorney that are important to you. Even the most experienced and skilled attorney is not right for every client. Ask yourself what it is that you are really looking for in an attorney so you can make your choice with these standards in mind.

It is important that you be confident in the attorney you hire. If you're unsure about whether the lawyer is really listening to you or understanding your concerns, keep looking until you find one who will. Your divorce is an important matter. It's critical that you have a professional you can trust.

3.3   Should I interview more than one attorney?

It is a good idea to interview more than one attorney. Every lawyer has different strengths, and it is important that you find the one that is right for you. Sometimes it is only by meeting with more than one attorney that you see clearly who will best be able to help you reach your goals. You might ask what kind of time frame a lawyer typically has for responding to calls or e-mails. Unless a lawyer is in trial, on vacation, or is ill, the lawyer should respond within twenty-four hours. Be wary of any lawyers who make promises regarding the outcome of your divorce.

Changing lawyers in the middle of litigation can be stressful and costly. It is wise to invest energy and time at the outset in making the right choice.

3.4 My spouse says because we're still friends we should use the same attorney for the divorce. Is this a good idea?

The most amicable of divorcing couples usually have differing interests. Even if you both agree to use one attorney, that attorney can have only one of you as his client. What most attorneys will do in this situation is, if it becomes a contested divorce or if the divorce will require litigation, they will withdraw from the case as they have learned things by meeting with both spouses that really make it unfair for the attorney to proceed in the case.

Sometimes, couples reach agreements without understanding all of their rights or what the law requires. A couple with children may indicate they have worked everything out, but the attorney for the party who is to receive the support may see that the number they have arrived at is less than what the Oklahoma Child Support Guidelines require. The attorney would explain that the judge will probably not sign off on that agreement.

It is not uncommon for one spouse to retain an attorney and for the other not to. In such cases, the spouse with the attorney files the petition, and agreements reached between the couple are typically sent to the other spouse for approval prior to any court hearing. If your spouse has filed for divorce and says that you do not need an attorney, you should still meet with a lawyer for advice and ask him or her to review any proposed divorce decree.

3.5 What information should I take with me to the first meeting with my attorney?

Attorneys differ on the amount of information they like to see at an initial consultation. If a court proceeding has already been initiated by either you or your spouse, it is important to take copies of any court documents.

If you have a prenuptial or antenuptial agreement with your spouse, that is another important document for you to share at the outset of your case.

If you intend to ask for support, either for yourself or for your children, documents showing proof of income for both you and your spouse will also be useful. These might include:

- Recent pay stubs
- Individual and business tax returns,W-2s, and 1099s
- Bank statements showing deposits
- A list of your assets and liabilities
- A statement of your monthly budget

If your situation is urgent or you do not have access to these documents, don't let it stop you from scheduling your appointment with an attorney. Prompt legal advice about your rights is often more important than having detailed financial information in the beginning.

Your attorney will ask you to complete a questionnaire or "intake" form at the time of your first meeting. Ask beforehand whether it is possible to do this in advance of your meeting. This can allow you time to provide more complete information and to make the most of your appointment time with the lawyer.

3.6 What unfamiliar words might an attorney use at the first meeting?

Law has a language all its own, and attorneys sometimes lapse into "legalese," forgetting that nonlawyers may not recognize words used daily in the practice of law. Some words and phrases you might hear include:

- *Dissolution of marriage*—the divorce
- *Petitioner*—the person who files the divorce petition
- *Respondent*—the person who did not file the divorce petition

- *Jurisdiction*—authority of a court to make rulings affecting a party
- *Process server*—the person who delivers legal papers that start the divorce
- *Discovery*—the process during which each side provides information to the other side
- *Decree*—the order that divorces the couple

Never hesitate to ask your attorney the meaning of a term. Your complete understanding of your lawyer's advice is essential.

3.7   What can I expect at an initial consultation with an attorney?

As mentioned, most attorneys will ask that you complete a questionnaire prior to the meeting. With few exceptions, attorneys are required to keep confidential all information you provide.

The nature of the advice you get from an attorney in an initial consultation will depend upon whether you are still deciding whether you want a divorce, are planning for a possible divorce in the future, or are ready to file for divorce right away.

During the meeting, you will have an opportunity to provide the following information to the attorney:

- A brief history of the marriage
- Background information regarding yourself, your spouse, and your children
- The overall financial situation of the marriage
- Your intentions and goals regarding your relationship with your spouse
- What information you are seeking from the attorney during the consultation
- What expectations or goals you have for the divorce

You can expect the attorney to provide the following information to you:

- A road map of the divorce process
- A preliminary list of the issues that he or she thinks will have an impact on the case

- An early assessment as to whether your expectations are reasonable or attainable
- Suggestions as to what you can work on to improve your situation
- How much the lawyer will charge for a retainer fee and his or her hourly rate

Although some of your questions may be impossible for the attorney to answer at the initial consultation because additional information or research is needed, the initial consultation is an opportunity for you to ask all of the questions you have at the time of the meeting.

3.8 Can I take a friend or family member to my initial consultation?

Yes. Having someone present during your initial consultation can be a source of support. You might ask him or her to take notes on your behalf so that you can focus on listening and asking questions. If you are the respondent spouse and did not expect the divorce, you may be in a state of shock. Having someone else present may provide you with a more objective version of what the lawyer said as opposed to what you believe was stated. Remember, however, that this is your consultation and it is important that the attorney hear the facts of your case directly from you.

3.9 What exactly will my attorney do to help me get a divorce?

You will be actively involved in some of the work during the divorce process, while other actions will be taken behind the scenes at the law office or the courthouse.

Your attorney may perform any of the following tasks on your behalf:

- Develop a strategy for advising you about all aspects of your divorce, including the treatment of assets and matters regarding children
- Prepare legal documents for filing with the court
- Conduct discovery to obtain information from the other party, which could include depositions, requests for production of documents, and written interrogatories

- Appear with you at all court appearances, depositions, and conferences
- Support you in responding to information requests from your spouse
- Inform you of actions you are required to take
- Perform financial analyses of your case
- Conduct legal research
- Prepare you for court appearances and depositions
- Prepare your case for hearings and trial, including preparing exhibits and interviewing witnesses
- Advise you about the judge's own preferences and temperament
- Counsel you regarding the risks and benefits of negotiated settlement as compared to proceeding to trial

3.10 What professionals might the court appoint to work with my attorney?

The attorneys may request and/or the court may appoint a *guardian ad litem (GAL)*. The GAL is an attorney or mental health professional whose duty it is to represent the best interest of the child. A guardian *ad litem* has the responsibility to investigate you and your spouse as well as the needs of your child. A GAL may then be called as a witness at trial to testify regarding any relevant observations. Most often, GALs are appointed in cases involving allegations that one or both of the parents are unfit or if there are allegations of physical or sexual abuse involving the children. In recent years the Oklahoma legislature has reduced the court fund, so in many cases you and your spouse likely will have to pay for the guardian *ad litem* fees.

Another expert that could be appointed is a *custody evaluator*. This is typically a psychologist or someone with at least a master's degree who performs certain mental health examinations of the parents. They will also interview the children. The custody evaluator usually will offer recommendations regarding custody and visitation. The judge is not required to follow the recommendations, but often the recommendations have a powerful impact on the judge's decision. Custody evaluators are not free and must be paid for by one or both of the spouses. If the custody evaluator is going to testify in court, as opposed to issuing a report, they will typically charge more than $5,000.

3.11 I've been divorced before, and I don't think I need an attorney this time; however, my spouse is hiring one. Is it wise to go it alone?

Having gone through a prior divorce, it's likely that you have learned a great deal about the divorce process as well as your legal rights. However, there are many reasons why you should be extremely cautious about proceeding without legal representation.

The length of the marriage, whether there are children, the relative financial situation for you and your spouse, as well as your age and health can all affect the financial outcome in your divorce.

The law may have changed since your last divorce. In some cases, the involvement of your lawyer could be minimal. This might be the case if your marriage was short, your financial situation is very similar to that of your spouse, there are no children, and the two of you remain amicable. At a minimum, have an initial consultation with an attorney to discuss your rights and have an attorney review any final agreement.

3.12 Can I take my children to meetings with my attorney?

No. Your attorney will be giving you a great deal of important information during your conferences, and it will benefit you to give your full attention.

It's also recommended that you take every measure to keep information about the legal aspects of your divorce away from your children. Knowledge that you are seeing an attorney can add to your child's anxiety about the process. It can also make your child a target for questioning by the other parent about your contacts with your attorney.

3.13 What is the role of the *paralegal* or *legal assistant* in my attorney's office?

A *paralegal,* or *legal assistant,* is a trained legal professional whose duties include providing support for you and your lawyer. Working with a paralegal can make your divorce easier because he or she is likely to be very available to help you. It can also lower your legal costs, as the hourly rate for paralegal services is less than the rate for attorneys.

A paralegal is prohibited from giving legal advice. It is important that you respect the limits of the role of the paralegal if he or she is unable to answer your question because it calls for giving a legal opinion. However, a paralegal can answer many questions and provide a great deal of information to you throughout your divorce.

Paralegals can help you by receiving information from you, reviewing documents with you, providing you with updates on your case, and answering questions about the divorce process that do not call for legal advice.

3.14   My attorney is not returning my phone calls or e-mails. What can I do?

You have a right to expect your phone calls to be returned by your lawyer. Here are some options to consider:

- Ask to speak to the paralegal or another attorney in the office.
- Send an e-mail or fax telling your lawyer that you have been trying to reach him or her by phone and explaining the reason it is important that you receive a call back.
- Ask the receptionist to schedule a phone conference for you to speak with your attorney at a specific date and time.
- Schedule a meeting with your attorney to discuss both the issue needing attention as well as your concerns about the communication.

3.15   How do I know when it's time to change lawyers?

Changing lawyers is costly. You will incur legal fees for your new attorney to review information that is already familiar to your current attorney. You will spend time giving much of the same information to your new lawyer as you gave to the attorney you have discharged. A change in lawyers often results in delays in the divorce.

The following are questions to ask yourself when you're deciding whether to stay with your attorney or seek new counsel:

- Have I spoken directly to my attorney about my concerns?
- When I expressed concerns, did my lawyer take action accordingly?
- Is my lawyer open and receptive to what I have to say?
- Am I blaming my lawyer for the bad behavior of my spouse or opposing counsel?
- Have I provided my lawyer with the information needed for taking the next action?
- Does my lawyer have control over the complaints I have, or are my complaints directed at a ruling the judge made that I don't like?
- Is my lawyer keeping promises for completing action on my case?
- Do I trust my lawyer?
- What would be the advantages of changing lawyers when compared to the costs?
- Do I believe my lawyer will support me to achieve the outcome I'm seeking in my divorce?

Every effort should be made to resolve challenges with your attorney. If you have made this effort and the situation remains unchanged, it may be time to switch lawyers.

4

Attorney Fees and Costs

The cost of your divorce might be one of your greatest concerns. Because of this, you will want to be an informed consumer of legal services. You want quality, but you also want to get the best value for the fees you are paying.

Divorce attorneys are paid based upon the amount of time they put into a case. At the outset of a case a lawyer has no way of answering one of your first questions, "How much is this going to cost me?" A lawyer cannot predict how many disagreements may occur between you and your spouse; accordingly, your attorney can tell you only what their retainer fee will be at the start of the case.

4.1 Can I get free legal advice from a lawyer over the phone?

Every law firm has its own policy regarding lawyers talking to people who are not yet clients of the firm. Most questions about your divorce are too complex for a lawyer to give a meaningful answer during a brief phone call.

4.2 Will I be charged for the initial consultation with a lawyer?

It depends. Some lawyers give free consultations, while others charge a fee. When scheduling your appointment, you should be told the amount of such a fee. Payment is ordinarily due at the time of the consultation.

4.3   Will I be expected to give money to the attorney after our first meeting? If so, how much?

If your attorney charges for an initial consultation, be prepared to make payment at the time of your meeting. At the close of your consultation, the attorney may also tell you the amount of the retainer needed by the law firm to handle your divorce. However, you are not expected to pay the retainer at the time of your first meeting. Rather, the retainer is paid after you have decided to hire the lawyer, the lawyer has accepted your case, and you are ready to proceed.

4.4   What exactly is a *retainer* and how much will mine be?

A *retainer* is a sum paid to your lawyer in advance for services to be performed and costs to be incurred in your divorce. If your lawyer does not use all of your retainer for whatever reason, the unused portion must be refunded to you.

If your case is accepted by the law firm, expect the attorney to request a retainer following the initial consultation. The amount of the retainer may vary from hundreds of dollars to several thousand dollars, depending upon the nature of your case. Contested custody, divorces involving a small business or abuse of the children, for example, are all likely to require higher retainers.

Other factors that can affect the amount of the retainer include the nature and number of the disputed issues, the degree of conflict between the parties, and the anticipated overall cost of the litigation.

4.5   I don't have any money and I need a divorce. What are my options?

If your income is low and your assets are few, you may be eligible to obtain a divorce at no cost or minimal cost through one of the following organizations:

- Oklahoma Legal Services (commonly referred to as *Legal Aid*)
- University of Oklahoma College of Law Legal Clinic
- Oklahoma City University School of Law Legal Clinic

These organizations have a screening process for potential clients, as well as limits on the nature of the cases they take. The demand for their services is greater than the number of attorneys available to handle cases. Consequently, if you are eligible for legal services from one of these programs, you should anticipate being on a waiting list. If you believe you might be eligible for participation in one of these programs, inquire early to increase your opportunity to get the legal help you are seeking.

In some cases, family and friends may be able to help you with the cost of your divorce.

4.6   I don't have much money, but I need to get a divorce as quickly as possible. What should I do?

If you have some money and want to get a divorce as soon as possible, consider some of these options:

- Borrow the legal fees.
- Charge the legal fees on a low-interest credit card.
- Talk with your attorney about using money held in a joint account with your spouse.
- Find an attorney who will work with you on a monthly payment basis.
- Ask your attorney about your spouse paying for your legal fees.

Even if you do not have the financial resources to proceed with your divorce at this time, consult with an attorney to learn your rights and to develop an action plan for steps you can take between now and the time you are able to proceed.

4.7   Is there anything I can do on my own to get support for my children if I don't have money for a lawyer?

Yes. If you need support for your children, contact the Oklahoma Department of Human Services Child Support Enforcement for help in obtaining a child-support order. Although they cannot help you with matters such as custody or property division, they can pursue support from your spouse for your children. Call toll free (800) 522-2922, or visit their website at www.okdhs.org.

4.8   How much does it cost to get a divorce?

I always tell my clients that the costs depend on many factors; neither I nor any other attorney can tell you exactly how much your divorce will cost. Ultimately it depends on how much time your lawyer puts into the case and whether any experts are utilized.

It is important that your discussion of the cost of your divorce begin at your first meeting with your attorney. As mentioned, it is customary for family law attorneys to request a retainer, also known as a *fee advance,* prior to beginning work on your case. The filing fee that the court clerk's office charges you to file the divorce petition (this assumes you initiate the divorce) is $210. In most cases serving your spouse with divorce documents by a process server ranges from $55 to $75 depending on how far away your spouse is and how easy it is for the process server to serve your spouse.

4.9   What are typical hourly rates for a divorce lawyer?

In Oklahoma, attorneys who practice in the divorce area usually charge from $150 to $400 an hour. The rate your attorney charges may depend upon factors such as legal skills, reputation, experience, and what other attorneys in the area are charging. Don't automatically assume because a lawyer charges a high hourly rate that she or he is a good divorce lawyer. I have known lawyers who are good in other areas of law, but handle only a few divorces and achieve mediocre results.

4.10   Can I make payments to my attorney?

Every law firm has its own policies regarding payment arrangements for divorce clients. Often these arrangements are tailored to the specific client. Most attorneys will require a substantial retainer to be paid at the outset of your case. Some attorneys may accept monthly payments in lieu of the retainer. Others may require monthly payments or request additional retainers as your case progresses.

4.11   I've been turned down by programs providing free legal services. How can I get the money to pay for a lawyer?

Some individuals find extra work to make money to pay for a lawyer. Or consider taking out a loan or charging your retainer on a credit card. Others get loans from family members and friends. Often, those close to you are concerned about your future and would be pleased to support you in your goal of having your rights protected. Although this may be uncomfortable to do, remember that most people will appreciate that you trusted them enough to ask for their help. If the retainer is too much money to request from a single individual, consider whether several people might each be able to contribute a lesser amount.

Under certain circumstances, an attorney might be willing to be paid from the proceeds of a property settlement. If you and your spouse have acquired substantial assets during the marriage, you may be able to find an attorney who will wait to be paid when the assets are divided at the conclusion of the divorce.

4.12 I agreed to pay my attorney a substantial retainer to begin my case. Will I still have to make monthly payments?

After you have exhausted your retainer agreement most attorneys are, at a minimum, going to expect you to make monthly payments on your balance. Some attorneys will require you to pay off your balance each month or they will stop representing you. Keep in mind your attorney has a rough idea of how much you owe, and you don't want your attorney worrying about whether you are going to pay them. You want them worrying about your case.

4.13 My lawyer gave me an estimate of the cost of my divorce and it sounds reasonable. Do I still need a written fee agreement?

Many good attorneys in Oklahoma do not provide a *written fee agreement*. Even if it is not their policy, you can ask them to provide you with a written agreement and almost all will comply.

A clear fee agreement reduces the risk of misunderstandings between you and your lawyer. It helps you both understand your responsibilities to each other so that your focus can be on the legal services being provided rather than on disputes about your fees.

4.14 How will I know how the fees and charges are accumulating?

Most attorneys will send you a monthly statement documenting their work, expenses, time spent, and the amount charged. Some attorneys will send a statement every two weeks.

Review the statement of your account promptly after you receive it. Check to make sure there are no errors, such as duplicate billing entries. If your statement reflects work that you were unaware was performed, call for clarification. Your statement might also include filing fees, court reporter fees for transcripts of court testimony or depositions, copy expenses, or interest charged on your account.

Legal fees can mount quickly and it's important that you stay aware of the status of your legal expenses. If four weeks have passed and you have not received a statement on your account, call your attorney's office to request one.

4.15 What other expenses are related to the divorce litigation besides lawyer fees?

Talk to your attorney about costs other than the attorney fees. Some typical fees consist of: filing fees (about $210 to start the divorce), court reporter transcript fees, subpoenas and mileage fees, and process server fees ($55 to $75). Ask how much the firm charges for copying costs and if they bill for postage. Expert-witness fees can be a substantial expense ranging from hundreds to thousands of dollars, depending upon the type of expert and the extent to which he or she is involved in your case.

Speak frankly with your attorney about these costs so that together you can make the best decisions about how to use your budget for the litigation.

4.16 Who pays for the experts such as appraisers, accountants, and psychologists?

Costs for the services of experts, whether appointed by the court or hired by the spouses, are paid for by the spouses.

In the case of the guardian *ad litem,* who may be appointed to represent the best interest of your children, the amount of the fee will depend upon how much time the professional spends. The judge often orders this fee to be divided by the couple, according to their child-support guideline percentage (see question 9.6 in chapter 9 about how the child-support percentage is calculated). However, depending upon the circumstances, one spouse can be ordered to pay the entire fee. If you can demonstrate low income and the court claim fund gets replenished, the state may pay the guardian *ad litem's* fees.

Psychologists charge either by the hour or can set a flat fee for a certain type of evaluation. Again, the court can order one spouse to pay this fee or for both to share the expense. It is not uncommon for a psychologist to request payment in advance or hold the release of an expert report until fees are paid.

The fees for many experts, including appraisers and accountants, will vary depending upon whether the individuals are called upon to provide only a specific service such as an appraisal, or if they will need to prepare for giving testimony and appear as a witness at trial.

4.17 What factors will impact how much my divorce will cost?

Although it is difficult to predict how much your legal fees will be, the following are some of the factors that affect the cost:

- Whether there are children; if so, are the children on SoonerCare (Oklahoma Medicaid)?
- Are you or your spouse generally inflexible?
- Is there a great deal of animosity between you and your spouse?
- Has child custody been agreed upon?
- Are there allegations involving substance abuse, gambling, addiction, or mental health issues?
- Is there a protective order or allegations of abuse?
- The hourly rate of your lawyer
- Whether there are litigation costs, such as fees for expert witnesses or court reporters

Keep in mind a lawyer is paid for his or her time, so if you contact your attorney frequently, you will incur a higher fee.

4.18   Will my attorney charge for phone calls and e-mails?

Yes. Many of the professional services provided by lawyers are done by phone and by e-mail. This time can be spent giving legal advice, negotiating, or gathering information to protect your interests. These calls and e-mails are all legal services for which you should anticipate being charged by your attorney.

To make the most of your time during attorney phone calls, plan your call in advance. Organize the information you want to relay, your questions, and any concerns to be addressed. This will help you to be clear and focused during the phone call so that your fees are well spent.

4.19   Will I be charged for talking to the staff at my lawyer's office?

Most lawyers and law firms with fewer than three lawyers will not bill for paralegal time; however, if you hire a larger firm, they probably will bill you.

Your lawyer's support staff will be able to relay your messages and receive information from you. They may also be able to answer some (but not all) of your questions. Don't expect a receptionist to give you an opinion regarding whether you will win custody or receive alimony. Allowing support from non-attorneys in the firm is one way to control your legal fees.

4.20   If my mother and father pay my legal fees, will my lawyer give them private information about my divorce?

If someone other than you is paying your legal bills, it is important that you are clear with your lawyer and with the persons paying that you expect your lawyer to honor their ethical duty to maintain confidentiality, assuming that is what you want.

Your lawyer will not be able to speak with your mother or father about the case outside of your presence unless you authorize this. However, if, for example, your parents come with you to meetings with your attorney and have other contacts with your attorney that you have authorized, your attorney is going to believe she or he can talk with them because you have consented to it. Don't give your attorney mixed messages. If you change your mind or you don't want your attorney to be able to speak with someone that you previously allowed them to speak with about the case, notify your attorney.

Understand that if your mother or father know about all aspects of the case and the other side is aware of this, your parents could potentially be put on the witness stand and asked about information that would otherwise be protected by attorney-client privilege.

4.21. Can I ask the court to order my spouse to pay my attorney fees?

Don't count on your spouse paying your attorney fees. This occurs only in a small percentage of cases. Typically, it requires the other side to engage in what the law calls *vexatious litigation* (the spouses acting very badly, dragging things out, and taking unreasonable positions). Understand that what you may consider as vexatious behavior on the part of your spouse, your judge may view as typical conduct in a contested divorce.

Attorney fees are awarded in less than 5 percent of divorce cases. Be very cautious if your lawyer tells you at any point in the case that she or he can get your attorney fees to be reimbursed by your spouse. If your lawyer tells you that they can get your spouse to reimburse you for your attorney fees, ask her or him to put that in writing. I predict at that point, the words "you misunderstood me" might come up.

4.22 What happens if I don't pay my attorney the fees I promised to pay?

The ethical rules for lawyers allow your attorney to withdraw from representation if you do not pay your attorney. Consequently, it is important that you keep the promises you have made regarding your account.

Above all, do not avoid communication with your attorney if you are having challenges making payment. Keeping in touch with your attorney is essential for you to have an advocate at all stages of your divorce.

4.23   Is there any way I can reduce some of the expenses of getting a divorce?

Litigation of any kind can be expensive, and divorces are no exception. The good news is that there are many ways that you can help to control the expense. Following are some of them.

Put it in writing. If you need to relay information that is important but not urgent, consider providing it to your attorney by mail, fax, or e-mail. This creates a prompt and accurate record for your file so that when your lawyer is getting your case ready for a hearing or trial it saves the lawyer time, which saves you money.

Organize your written information. Whether it is copies of text messages, copies of checks for child support, or financial records, try to put these documents in some type of chronological order and segregate documents of different types with paper clips before dropping them off at your lawyer's office. You would be amazed how many clients drop off boxes of files that have been mixed together and have no chronological order.

Keep your attorney informed. Just as your attorney should keep you up to date on the status of your case, you need to do the same. Keep your lawyer advised about any major developments in your life such as plans to move or to obtain a new job. It is always better have your lawyer find out from you that you have begun dating than to discover while you are on the witness stand that you have begun dating someone else and have allowed that person to be around your children. If you have a doubt as to whether something is important, it is better to err on the side of caution and to let your attorney know about it at the outset.

During a divorce, your address, phone number, or e-mail address may change. Be sure to let your attorney know. You would be amazed how many people in this hectic period forget to notify their own attorney of the change. Often, timely advice on the part of your lawyer can avoid the need for more costly fees later.

Obtain copies of documents. An important part of litigation includes reviewing documents such as tax returns, account statements, report cards, or medical records. Your attorney will ordinarily be able to request or subpoena these items, but many may be readily available to you directly upon request.

Utilize support professionals. Get to know the support staff at your lawyer's office. The receptionist, paralegal, legal secretary, or law clerk may be the person who has the answer to your question. Only the attorneys in the office are able to give you legal advice, but other professionals in the law office can often provide the answers to questions regarding the status of your case. Just as your communication with your attorney, all communication with any professionals in a law firm is required to be kept strictly confidential.

Consider working with an associate attorney. Although the senior attorneys or partners in a law firm may have more experience, you may find that working with an associate attorney is a good option. Hourly rates for an associate attorney are typically lower than those charged by a senior partner. Frequently, the associate attorney has trained under a senior partner and developed excellent skills as well as knowledge of the law. Many associate attorneys are also very experienced.

Leave a detailed message. If your attorney knows what information you are seeking, she or he can often get the answer before returning your call. This not only gets your answer faster, but also reduces costs.

Discuss more than one matter during a call. It is not unusual for clients to have many questions during litigation. If your question is not urgent, consider waiting to call until you have more than one inquiry. Never hesitate to call to ask any legal questions.

Provide timely responses to information request. Whenever possible, provide information requested by your lawyer in a timely manner. This avoids the cost of follow-up action by your lawyer and the additional expense of extending the time in litigation.

Carefully review your monthly statements. Scrutinize your monthly billing statements closely. If you believe an error has been made, contact your lawyer's office right away to discuss your concerns.

Remain open to settlement. Be alert to when your disagreement with your spouse is about smaller sums of money that will often cost more in legal fees to take to court than the value of what is disputed. Are you fighting over a real issue or is it because you want to hurt your spouse?

By doing your part, you can use your legal fees wisely and control the costs of your divorce.

5

The Discovery Process

Interrogatories. Depositions. *Subpoena duces tecum.* Requests for production of documents and requests for admissions. It sounds intimidating, doesn't it?

The purpose of discovery is to ensure that both you and your spouse have access to the same information. This way, you can either negotiate a fair agreement or have all of the facts and documents to present to the judge at trial.

Discovery is that part of your divorce process in which the attorneys attempt to learn as much about the facts of your case as possible. Through a variety of methods, both lawyers will request information from you, your spouse, and potential witnesses in your case. Information may be requested from third parties such as employers, banks, and retirement management companies.

There is no doubt that the discovery process can be burdensome because of the need to obtain and to provide lots of detailed information. Completing it, however, can provide tremendous clarity about the issues in your divorce. Remember the old adage "Failure to prepare is preparing to fail." This adage is absolutely spot on for the discovery process.

5.1 What types of discovery might be done by my lawyer or my spouse's lawyer?

Types of discovery include:

- *Interrogatories*—written questions that must be answered under oath

51

- *Requests for production of documents*—asking that certain documents be provided by you or your spouse
- *Requests for admissions*—asking that certain facts be admitted or denied
- *Subpoena of documents*
- *Depositions*—in which questions are asked and answered in the presence of a court reporter but outside of the presence of a judge

Factors that can influence the type of discovery conducted in your divorce can include:

- The types of issues in dispute
- How much access you and your spouse have to needed information
- The level of cooperation between you and your spouse in sharing information
- The budget available for performing discovery

5.2   How long does the discovery process take?

Discovery can take anywhere from thirty days to many months, depending upon factors such as the complexity of the case, the cooperation of you and your spouse, and whether expert witnesses are involved.

If you or your spouse is self-employed, in most cases discovery is going to take longer because there are issues over how much income is generated by the business and what is the value of the business.

5.3   My lawyer insists that we conduct discovery, but I don't want to spend the time and money on it. Is it really necessary?

The discovery process can be critical to a successful and fair outcome in your case for several reasons:

- It increases the likelihood that any agreements reached are based on accurate information.
- It provides necessary information for deciding whether to settle or go to trial.
- It supports the preparation of defenses by providing information regarding your spouse's case.

- It avoids surprises at trial, such as unexpected witness testimony.
- It oftentimes provides a better overall picture of the assets and liabilities.

In many marriages one spouse handles the money and the other spouse often does not have a good understanding of all of the debts and assets. There may be more assets or debts than you realize and the discovery process is the only way to determine a complete financial picture. At a minimum, allow your lawyer to send out some written discovery requests; this should not be too costly. Remember, if you handicap your lawyer you ultimately are harming your case.

5.4 I just received from my spouse's attorney interrogatories and requests that I produce documents. My lawyer wants me to respond within two weeks. I'll never make the deadline. What can I do?

Do not stick the discovery papers in a drawer and tell yourself you will come back to it next week. If you do this it is almost a certainty you will not follow up. If you know that you are a procrastinator, call your attorney's legal assistant and ask him or her to put it on their calendar to encourage you to respond to questions. The following are steps you can take to make this task easier:

- First, look at all of the questions. Many of them will not apply to you, or your answers will be a simple "yes" or "no."
- Ask a friend to help you. It is important that you develop the practice of letting others help you while you are going through your divorce. Break tasks down into smaller sections. If you answer just a few questions a day, the job will not be so overwhelming.
- Call your lawyer. Ask whether a paralegal in the office can help you organize the needed information or determine whether some of it can be provided at a later date.

Delay in the discovery process often leads to frustration by clients and lawyers.

5.5   My spouse's lawyer intends to subpoena my medical records. Aren't these private?

Whether or not your medical records are relevant in your case will depend upon the issues in dispute. If you are requesting alimony or if your health is an issue in a dispute over child custody, these records may be used.

It may be that a motion to stop the subpoena, known as a *motion to quash,* is needed—or the nature of the records that can be obtained should be limited to those relevant to your divorce.

5.6   It's been two months since my lawyer sent interrogatories to my spouse, and we still don't have his answers. I answered mine on time. Is there anything that can be done to speed up the process?

Talk with your attorney about filing a motion to compel, seeking a court order that your spouse provide the requested information by a certain date. A request for attorney fees for the filing of the motion may also be appropriate.

Ask your lawyer whether a subpoena of information from an employer or a financial institution would be a more cost-effective way to get needed facts and documents if your spouse remains uncooperative.

5.7   What is a *deposition?*

A *deposition* is the asking and answering of questions under oath, in the presence of a court reporter who later prints a transcript of the session. A deposition may be taken of you, your spouse, or potential witnesses in your divorce case, including experts. Both attorneys will be present. You and your spouse have the right to be present during the taking of depositions of any witnesses in your case.

Depositions are not performed in most divorces. They are most common in cases involving contested custody, persons with higher income, and expert witnesses.

5.8   What is the purpose of a deposition?

A deposition can serve a number of purposes, such as:

- Providing new information or clarifying information that you already have

- Aiding in the assessment of a witness's credibility, that is, whether the witness appears to be telling the truth
- Helping avoid surprise at trial by learning the testimony of witnesses in advance
- Preserving testimony in the event the witness becomes unavailable for trial

Depositions can be essential tools in a divorce, especially when a case is likely to proceed to trial. Remember, when your deposition is being taken, it is not the time to try and "win" your case. It's not the time to show your intellect or argue with your spouse's attorney. A deposition involves you answering questions from your spouse's attorney. Simply answer the questions as best as you can.

5.9 Will what I say in my deposition be used against me when we go to court?

It can be. Primarily it could be used to *impeach* you. This means if during a hearing or the divorce trial, you testify to something that appears to be different from what you said in the deposition, your spouse's lawyer will ask you about this difference and suggest you are not being truthful. There may be a clear reason for this, such as you filed your petition and requested joint custody and testified about that in the deposition, but since that time you discovered that you and your spouse are having difficulty working with one another over what is best for the children. Under such a scenario, your answer has changed because of a change in circumstances, not because you contradicted yourself.

I would recommend that you review your deposition transcript immediately upon receipt of it and do not to wait until the night before trial to read your transcript for the first time.

5.10 Will the judge read the depositions?

Only in rare cases would a judge read an entire deposition transcript. One extreme example might be if one of the parties becomes unavailable at the time of trial. Generally speaking, the judge is going to see only small selected portions of the deposition.

5.11   How should I prepare for my deposition?

To prepare for your deposition, review the important documents in your case. Look over the petition; any pleadings in which you requested some type of relief, such as an application for a temporary order; your answers to interrogatories; and any financial documents your lawyer has submitted to the other lawyer.

You will intuitively know some of the important questions you are going to be asked. If you are in a contested custody over the children, you know that you will be asked some version of this question, "Why is it in the best interest of your children that you be awarded custody of them?" Planning ahead and not winging the answer to a crucial question such as this is of paramount importance. If you answer this question by attacking your spouse, you will likely come off as being vindictive and more concerned about settling the score rather than doing what is best for your children.

Talk to your attorney about the types of questions you can expect to be asked.

5.12   Can I refuse to answer questions?

The basic rule is if you are asked a question you will need to answer it. If there is an objection by your attorney, say nothing until the attorneys discuss the objection. Unless your attorney directly tells you not to answer the question, you will need to answer the question.

The attorney is allowed to ask anything that is reasonably calculated to lead to the discovery of admissible evidence. Many questions that are asked in a deposition cannot be asked at trial, so understand that in many cases the questions may seem to get far afield from what you think matters.

Note that if you appear uncomfortable with a question or try to avoid answering your spouse's lawyer, he or she will notice this. Your spouse's attorney may push the issue; he or she may be trying to "rattle" you and see how you react to things that make you uncomfortable. If you do become rattled while being questioned by your spouse's attorney, he or she may believe he can discourage you from taking the case to trial.

Even though a question may bother you, try to not let the other lawyer know this because they will likely stick on the topic longer if they see it is upsetting you.

5.13 What if I give incorrect information in my deposition?

A *deposition* is a formal judicial proceeding testimony taken under oath from a witness (also known as the *deponent*) that carries with it the penalties of perjury. At the end of your deposition, you will be asked whether you want to review and sign your deposition or waive that right. Waiving it means you agree with everything the court reporter is going to type up and that you have no changes to the answers to any questions you were asked.

I recommend you review and sign the deposition transcript after it is produced a few weeks later. This will give you the opportunity to correct, to a limited degree, any details you might have forgotten about or felt you did not do a good job explaining. You would put this information on an errata sheet and send it back to the court reporter, who would in turn add the errata sheet and mail it to the lawyers in the case. Consult with your lawyer before sending back the errata sheet. Depending on the amount of changes you may make, you may be deposed again on those changes.

5.14 What happens if I lie at my deposition?

If you lie during your deposition, you risk being impeached by the other lawyer during your divorce trial. Lying, whether it is in a deposition or in a court hearing, is bad for you for reasons beyond just having to worry about being impeached or committing perjury. In most contested divorces, there are multiple areas in which the two spouses' testimony is clearly in conflict with each other. Assume you have an example in which your spouse says "It is black," and you say "It's white." If one party has been impeached, which party do you think the judge is going to believe?

5.15 What if I don't know or can't remember the answer to a question?

You may be asked questions about which you have no knowledge. If you truly do not know or cannot recall, you can state that. Keep in mind, whether in a deposition or in trial, that if you chronically use the "I don't know" or "I don't recall" responses you are going to create a question about your overall credibility. If your lack of ability to recall appears to apply to areas that may cast you in an unfavorable light, it casts doubt on your credibility.

If there is a topic about which you are not 100 percent sure, but you're fairly confident, you could say something like "I am not 100 percent certain, but I have a high degree of confidence that my wife has not attended a parent teacher's conference in three years." Or you could say, "I have a strong belief that Tom has not paid for extracurricular activities since our son was in sixth grade."

5.16 Can I speak about something that has not been asked of me?

It is human nature to want to tell your story. Some people have a hard time not telling their story when they are asked specific questions. You do not want to be what the law calls a "nonresponsive witness." This means you are not answering the specific question asked, but are providing an answer to a question that has not been asked. This is a fairly common problem. You'll want to avoid it.

Here is an example: If you are asked whether you spent the 2015 income tax return money to buy a used car and you respond that your spouse spent the 2016 tax return money on his business, you are being nonresponsive. You were not asked what your husband did or what happened with the 2016 return, you were asked about the 2015 income tax money. Before your deposition, ask a friend to ask you practice questions to make sure you are being responsive.

5.17 What else do I need to know about having my deposition taken?

Prepare for your deposition by reviewing and providing necessary documents and talking with your lawyer. The following suggestions will help you to give a successful deposition:

- Arrive early for your deposition so that you have time to get comfortable with your surroundings.

- Take slow, deep breaths. It will help you relax. You are going to be asked questions about matters you know. Your deposition is likely to begin with routine matters such as your educational and work history.
- Be aware that the lawyer conducting the deposition *cannot* ask you what you and your attorney spoke about to prepare for the deposition. Such information is attorney-client privileged information.
- Stay calm. Your spouse's lawyer will be judging your credibility and demeanor.
- Do not argue with the attorneys.
- Listen carefully to the entire question. Do not try to anticipate questions or start thinking about your answer before the attorney has finished asking the question.
- Answer the question directly. If the question calls only for "yes" or "no," provide such an answer.
- Do not volunteer information. If the lawyer wants to elicit more information, he or she will do so in follow-up questions.
- If you do not understand the question clearly, ask that it be repeated or rephrased. Do not try to answer what you *think* was asked.
- Take your time and carefully consider the question before answering. There is no need to hurry. It is best to keep your pace slow throughout.
- If you do not know or cannot remember the answer, say so.
- If your answer is an estimate or approximation, say so. Do not let an attorney pin you down to anything you are not sure about.
- If the attorney mischaracterizes something you said earlier, say so.
- If the attorney starts off his or her question with an assertion that you do not agree with, begin your answer by stating you don't agree with the assertion. For example, if you are asked, "Were you drunk on the Fourth of July when you got into a fight with your

wife in front of the children?" You might begin your answer by responding, "I was not drunk on the Fourth of July."

- If you need a break at any point in the deposition, you have the right to request one. You can talk to your attorney during such a break, but you will need to answer the pending question before a break.

5.18   Are depositions always necessary? Must every witness be deposed?

No. In most divorce cases, depositions are not taken. The majority of divorces in Oklahoma occur without anyone being deposed. They are more likely to be needed in cases involving child custody or in which there are substantial assets or incomes. Although depositions of all witnesses are usually unnecessary, it is common to take the depositions of expert witnesses if you have any.

6

Mediation and Negotiation

Most of the local court rules in Oklahoma now require you and your spouse to attend mediation before a judge will set a divorce trial date. So, in most cases, you are going to mediation whether or not you want to. There are two primary reasons for the increased use of mediation. The first is that judges would rather you and your spouse work out your differences by agreement rather than have a decision forced upon you by the judge. The second reason is that judges are extremely busy, and if they can have someone else, namely the mediator, settle a case, they are satisfied.

6.1 What is the difference between *mediation* and *negotiation?*

Both mediation and negotiation are methods used to help you and your spouse settle your divorce by reaching agreement rather than going to trial and having the judge make decisions for you. These methods are sometimes referred to as *alternative dispute resolution* or *ADR*.

Mediation uses a trained mediator who is an independent, neutral third party. You can conduct mediation with or without your attorneys. *Negotiation* typically means lawyers for both you and your spouse are trying to reach an agreement.

6.2 Are all mediators lawyers?

Mediators are not required to be lawyers, but the majority of mediators are lawyers. If you have complex property issues, it makes sense to utilize a mediator who is an attorney. On the other hand, if you are primarily just trying to work out a visitation schedule for your children, you could utilize a mediator who is not an attorney and get equally good results, typically with a lower fee.

6.3   Who pays for mediation and how much do mediators charge?

Typically, each side pays half of the mediator's fees. Only in rare cases does one spouse pay the entire fee. If you hire an attorney to mediate your dispute, most will charge between $175 and $300 an hour with each side usually paying at the start of the mediation for one hour of the mediator's time. The attorney will charge you for her or his time for the mediation. If you hire a non-attorney mediator, the costs are usually in the $100 an hour range.

There is a statewide mediation program called Early Settlement Mediation Programs. You can obtain additional information by going to www.oscn.net/static/adr/Documents/ADRS_Directory.pdf or by calling (405) 522-7876. The Early Settlement programs offer mediation services for approximately $5 from each side, and they do an excellent job. Typically, these programs are utilized by people with limited incomes. Some of their mediators are lawyers or law students.

6.4   What is involved in the mediation process? What will I have to do and how long will it take?

Most mediators will send you a packet in advance of mediation to obtain some basic information and to provide you with guidelines about the mediation. It is common for attorneys to attend mediations. Typically, if one party's attorney attends, the other party's attorney will also.

At the start of the mediation, the mediator will outline ground rules designed to ensure that you will be treated respectfully and given an opportunity to be heard. Every mediator conducts their mediations differently. If there are protective orders or great hostility, the mediator will keep you and your spouse in separate rooms. If you feel intimated by your spouse or don't feel it will be productive to be in the same room, you can request that the mediator seat you in separate rooms. Be advised that this makes the process more difficult because the mediator has to travel back and forth and, for some reason, this separation often emboldens some people to be more difficult and less flexible.

Typically, the mediation itself will last two to four hours. A second or follow-up mediation can occur, if needed.

6.5 How can mediation and negotiation lower the costs of my divorce?

If your case is not settled by agreement, you will be going to trial. If you are fighting over a lot of issues, such as custody, property division, and alimony, the costs of going to trial will be expensive.

Even if you do not settle the entire case through mediation or negotiation, you can settle a portion of your case and it will save you money. For example, if you settle visitation and custody, but not the property issues, you will have saved a substantial amount in attorney's fees when the case goes to trial.

By settling your case without going to trial, you may be able to save thousands of dollars in legal fees. Ask your attorney for a litigation budget that outlines the potential costs of going to trial. This will give you an idea of these costs when deciding whether to settle an issue or to take it to trial before a judge.

6.6 Are there other benefits to mediating or negotiating a settlement?

Yes. A divorce resolved by a mediated or negotiated agreement can have these additional benefits:

Reduces the risk of leaving scars on both sides. Unfortunately, in most contested divorce cases, one or both sides will bring up matters that often create very hard feelings that last beyond the courtroom. If you have children, you will need to interact with your former spouse on a weekly basis for many years. If, for example, you testify at trial that your spouse drinks too much, and he testifies that you are difficult to deal with, it may create hard feelings later, when you are attempting to discuss matters related to your children. Causing ill will with your spouse can be harmful to your children. They know when you are fighting whether you realize it or not.

Recognizes common goals. Looking at all possible solutions often leads to creative solutions to common goals. For example, suppose you and your spouse both agree that you need to pay your spouse some amount of equity for the family home you will keep, but you have no cash to make the payment. Together, you might come up with a number of options for accomplishing your goal and select the best one. Contrast this with a judge who could simply order the house to be sold and the proceeds to be divided.

Addresses the unique circumstances of your situation. Rather than using a one-size-fits-all approach, as a judge might do, a settlement reached by agreement allows you and your spouse to consider the unique circumstances of your situation. This allows you to formulate a good outcome. For example, suppose you disagree about the parenting times for the Thanksgiving holiday. The judge might order you to alternate the holiday each year, even though you both would have preferred to have your child share the day with both parents.

Fulfills your children's needs. You may see that your children would be better served by you and your spouse deciding their future rather than having it decided by a judge who does not know, love, and understand your children like the two of you do.

Eliminates the risk and uncertainty of trial. If a judge decides the outcome of your divorce, you give up control over the terms of the settlement. The decisions are left in the hands of the judge. If you and your spouse reach agreement, however, you can eliminate the risk of an uncertain outcome. All lawyers and their clients have had outcomes that surprised them.

Lowers stress. The process of preparing for and going to court can be stressful. Your energy should be going toward caring for your children, watching your finances, and coping with the emotions of divorce. You might decide that you would be better served by settling your case rather than proceeding to trial.

Achieves closure. When you are going through a divorce, the process can feel as though it is taking an eternity. By reaching agreement, you and your spouse are better able to put the divorce behind you and move forward with your lives.

6.7 How are *mediation* and *negotiation* different from a *collaborative divorce*?

Collaborative law is a method of resolving a divorce case in which both parties have a strong commitment to settling their disputes and avoiding litigation. You and your spouse each hire an attorney trained in the collaborative law process. Your lawyers enter into an agreement that provides that, in the event either you or your spouse decides to take the case to court, both of you must terminate services with your collaborative lawyers and start anew.

Very few divorces are resolved this way. This process requires that both spouses are willing to compromise on all issues. Keep in mind, in most cases people are getting divorced because they do not get along.

6.8 Is mediation mandatory?

In many counties in Oklahoma, it is now mandatory through local court rules that, before a divorce trial date will be set, mediation must occur.

6.9 My spouse abused me and I am afraid to participate in mediation. Should I participate anyway?

If you have been a victim of domestic violence by your spouse, it is important that you discuss this with your attorney. Mediation may not be a safe way for you to reach agreement. If the court rule in your county requires mediation, talk to your attorney about whether seeking a waiver of mediation is an appropriate option. If you have a protective order, the mediator will keep you in different rooms during the mediation.

Mediators should ask you whether you have been a victim of domestic violence prior to allowing mediation to proceed. This is critical for the mediator to both assess your safety and to ensure that the balance of power in the mediation process is maintained.

6.10 What training and credentials do mediators have?

The background of mediators varies. As mentioned earlier, most—but not all—mediators are attorneys. Most attorneys will only send their clients to mediators who are attorneys. In order to be a certified mediator, the mediator must have had forty hours of specialized training.

6.11 What types of issues can be mediated or negotiated?

All of the issues in your case can be mediated or negotiated. However, in advance of any mediation or negotiation session, you should discuss with your lawyer whether there are issues that you do not want to be negotiated.

6.12 How do I prepare for mediation?

Prior to attending a mediation session with your spouse, discuss with your attorney the issues you intend to mediate. In particular, be sure to discuss the impact of custody and parenting time arrangements on child support.

Think a few steps ahead. Have a detailed list of proposed property division, including property values.

6.13 Do children attend the mediation sessions?

Children will almost never attend mediation. This avoids having the children be put in the middle of the dispute. In unusual circumstances, if both sides agree, children could attend, but this would require a very compelling reason.

6.14 I want my attorney to look over the agreements my spouse and I discussed in mediation before I give my final approval. Is this possible?

Yes. Before giving your written or final approval to any agreements reached in mediation, it is critical that your attorney review the agreements first. This is necessary to ensure that you understand the terms of the settlement and its implications. If you are planning on attending the mediation without your attorney, let him or her know that you would like to reach them by phone during the mediation to see if your attorney thinks the potential agreement is fair. You would need to plan this with your attorney in advance.

6.15 What if mediation fails?

If mediation is not successful, you still may be able to settle your case through negotiations between the attorneys. Also, you and your spouse can agree to preserve the settlements that were reached and to take only the remaining disputed issues to the judge for trial.

6.16 What is a *settlement conference?*

A *settlement conference* is a meeting held with you, your spouse, and your lawyers with the intention of negotiating the terms of your divorce. With the advent of mediation, settlement conferences have dramatically declined. In the past these conferences would oftentimes involve a judge who is not assigned to your case, but who attempts to strongly urge the parties to reach an agreement. Generally speaking, you are not going to get a settlement conference in a divorce case.

6.17 Why is my lawyer appearing so friendly with my spouse and her lawyer?

Lawyers are professionals who are respectful or pleasant toward your spouse or your spouse's lawyer to promote a good outcome for you.

6.18 What happens if my spouse and I settled some but not all of the issues in our divorce?

You and your spouse can agree to maintain the agreements you have reached and let the judge decide those matters that you are unable to resolve. Also, if you have narrowed the issues down, you can request an advisory opinion. If you and your spouse have everything resolved except a few minor issues, the two lawyers can tell the judge what issue or issues are unresolved. The judge would then listen to each of the lawyer's arguments and tell them what he or she would likely do if these issues were presented at trial. At that point, the two lawyers tell their clients what the judge said and typically both sides understand there is no use in arguing in court. Instead, they implement the judge's advisory opinion into the divorce decree.

6.19 If my spouse and I reach an agreement, how long will it take before we can go before the judge to have it approved at a final hearing?

In most cases, if a settlement is reached through negotiation or mediation, one of the attorneys will put the agreement in writing within a week. Oftentimes, there is some back and forth over minor changes or clarifications between the attorneys. Once both sides and their attorneys have signed the decree, some judges will simply sign it in their *chambers* (the judge's office outside of the courtroom) and give it back to the attorneys to file in the court clerk's office. Other judges will require at least one party and their attorney to provide testimony to establish jurisdiction, and then the judge will sign it. It should be done within three weeks.

7

Domestic Violence and Victim Protective Orders

Domestic violence is something that has generated an enormous amount of attention and action by the legal system. When spouses, intimate partners, dates, or family members use physical violence, threats, emotional abuse, harassment, or stalking to control the behavior of their partners, they are committing domestic violence. Most victims of domestic violence are women. Children who witness domestic violence can also be victims; studies have shown such violence can impact their future behavior as adults. Judges in Oklahoma are required to attend a mandatory course on domestic violence. Unfortunately, false allegations of abuse to gain an advantage in the divorce process are an all-too-common problem.

7.1   I'm afraid my abusive spouse will try to hurt me and/or our children. What resources are available to help me?

Develop a plan with your safety and that of your children as your highest priority. In addition to meeting with an attorney at your first opportunity, develop a safety plan in the event you and your children need to escape your home.

An effective way to do this is to let in support from an agency that helps victims of domestic violence. Contact your local Domestic Violence Intervention Service (DVIS) www.domesticshelters.org. You can also call the Oklahoma Coalition Against Domestic Violence and Sexual Assault (405) 524-0700. The Oklahoma Department of Human Services (see Resources at the end of this book) has produced an excellent booklet entitled *Domestic Violence Awareness Guide* that provides information and resources.

7.2 I am afraid to meet with a lawyer because I am terrified my spouse will find out and get violent. What should I do?

Schedule an initial consultation with an attorney who is experienced in working with domestic violence victims. Consultations with your attorney are confidential. Your lawyer has an ethical duty to not disclose details of your meeting with anyone outside of the law firm. Let your attorney know your concerns so that extra precautions can be taken by the law office in handling your file.

7.3 I want to give my attorney all the information needed so my children and I are safe from my spouse. What should I provide?

Provide your attorney with complete information about the history, background, and nature of the abuse. Evidence may include:

- The types of abuse (for example, physical, sexual, verbal, financial, mental, emotional)
- The dates, time frames, or occasions
- The locations
- Whether you were ever treated medically
- Any police reports made
- E-mails, letters, notes, or journal entries
- Any photographs taken
- Any witnesses to the abuse or evidence of the abuse
- Any statements made by your spouse admitting the abuse
- Any damaged property
- Injuries you or your children suffered
- Any counseling you had because of the abuse
- Alcohol or drug abuse
- The presence of guns or other weapons

7.4 What is a *victim protective order* or protective order and how can I get one?

A *victim protective order* (also called a *protective order*) is a court order that may offer a number of protections, including granting you temporary custody of your children and ordering your spouse to leave the family residence and have no contact with you. If your spouse violates the protective order he or she can be charged with a crime.

A protective order may be obtained without an attorney. You can go to the court clerk's office and request paperwork for the order. A protective order can be requested on an emergency or non-emergency basis, however the overwhelming majority are granted on an emergency basis. A protective order can also be obtained on behalf of children.

An emergency protective order can be granted without your spouse being present. Typically, you will not give testimony. The clerk takes a copy of your petition for a protective order and a judge reviews it. If he or she finds there are sufficient allegations of domestic abuse, an immediate order of protection will be granted.

If you obtain an emergency protective order, your spouse will be served with notice by a sheriff's deputy. A protective order hearing must be set within ten days of the date that the emergency protective order is granted. Your spouse can appear at the hearing with or without an attorney. At that point, you will need to provide testimony on the need for the protective order to continue. You may call witnesses if you have any, and your spouse or his or her attorney can ask you questions about your testimony. Your spouse will, in most cases, also testify and provide a different version of how the events unfolded and may have his or her own witnesses.

After hearing the evidence, the judge will make a ruling as to whether to continue the protective order. If your spouse fails to appear or if he or she has not been served with notice, typically the protective order will be continued for some period of time, depending on the particular judge.

7.5 What's the difference between a *protective order* and a *restraining order*?

Protective orders and restraining orders are both court orders directing a person to not engage in certain behaviors. *Protective orders* apply to people, usually a spouse, boyfriend, girlfriend, or possibly a family member. As it relates to divorce and custody, you would almost always be dealing with a protective order and not a restraining order.

Restraining orders may or may not apply to people. A restraining order may apply to a company or something business-related. For example, the Love Me Tender Wedding Chapel in Las Vegas could be restrained from selling Elvis Presley figurines.

7.6 My spouse says I am crazy, that I am a liar, and that no judge will ever believe me if I tell the truth about the abusive behavior. What can I do if I don't have any proof?

Most domestic violence is not witnessed by third parties. Often there is little physical evidence. Even without physical evidence, a judge can enter orders to protect you and your children if you give truthful testimony about your abuse that the judge finds believable. Your own testimony of your abuse is evidence. See question 7.4.

It is very common for persons who abuse others to claim that their victims are liars and to make statements intended to discourage disclosure of the abuse. This is yet another form of controlling behavior. Your attorney's skills and experience will support you in giving effective testimony in the courtroom to establish your case.

7.7 My spouse told me that if I ever file for divorce, I'll never see my child again. Should I be worried about my child being abducted?

Your fear that your spouse will abduct your child is a common one. Know that although threats of taking a child away are not uncommon, it is fairly unusual for a parent to actually act on the threat. If an abduction does occur, you should report it to law enforcement immediately. They can implement an Amber alert. If the Amber alert system goes into effect, resources are put into place and make it likely your child will be returned soon.

Virtual brainwashing is almost always present in cases in which a child is at risk for being kidnapped by a parent. Efforts to isolate the child from friends and family may also be seen. Exit activities such as obtaining a new passport, getting financial matters in order, or contacting a moving company could be indicators.

Talk to your lawyer to assess the risks in your particular case. Together you can determine whether statements by your spouse are threats intended to control or intimidate you or whether legal action is needed to protect your child.

7.8 How does consolidating the protective order into the divorce case affect the hearing for a protection order?

If your spouse has already obtained an emergency protective order against you, the court will set a hearing within ten days; you can attend this hearing and provide your side of the story. However, if either party files a divorce petition after the protective order has been filed, and they also request a temporary hearing, the two hearings will be combined into one. This means a delay of the protective order hearing. During this time, the spouse with the protective order against him or her (statistically speaking, it is most often the husband) will not be able to go to the marital residence or see the children.

7.9 How disadvantaged are you if your spouse has a protective order against you?

If you find yourself in the position of having a protective order entered against you, understand that you are operating under a disability. You are not allowed to contact your spouse. Don't inflame the situation by sending your spouse threatening texts or e-mails. This can lead to criminal charges being filed against you. Even if your spouse initiates a call or text, you must not respond.

Keep in mind that protective orders are typically entered early in a divorce process and this gives you time to demonstrate that the protective order should not have been entered and show what steps you have taken to address the problem. If, for example, you did not have an attorney at the time the protective order hearing occurred, you can ask your attorney to file a motion to vacate (dismiss) the protective order later on if you have new facts or evidence or things have changed.

This is going to be an extremely frustrating time, especially if you cannot see your children except under supervised visitation. Work on a plan with your attorney's guidance to get the protective order dismissed. Think before you act so you don't have criminal charges filed against you.

7.10 What legal steps can be taken to prevent my spouse from removing our child from the state?

If you are concerned about your child being removed from the state, talk to your lawyer about whether any of these options might be available in your case:

- A court order giving you immediate custody until a temporary custody hearing can be held
- Supervised visitation

Both state and federal laws are designed to provide protection from the removal of children from one state to another when a custody matter is ongoing. The *Uniform Child Custody Jurisdiction Enforcement Act (UCCJEA)* was passed to encourage the custody of children to be decided in the state where they have been living most recently and where they have the most ties. The *Parental Kidnapping Prevention Act (PKPA)* makes it a federal crime for a parent to violate a custody order by kidnapping a child.

8

Child Custody

If you have custody of your children, their well-being is likely your number one concern in the divorce process. No matter what happens, the amount of time you spend with your children is going to be changed by the divorce. You cannot control this fact. However, you can control your relationship with your children.

It can be difficult not to worry about how sharing parenting time with your spouse will affect your children. You may also have fears about being cut out of your child's life. Try to remember that, regardless of who has custody, it is likely that the court order will not only give you a decent amount of time with your children but you also will be able to attend school functions and their other activities.

8.1   What types of custody are awarded in Oklahoma?

Under Oklahoma law, there are two types of custody. One type provides that one parent has legal custody and he or she makes all of the child's major decisions. This is called *full custody*. The other type of custody is *joint custody* where the decision making is shared.

Historically, time spent with the noncustodial parent has been referred to as *visitation*. Today the term time share is used to refer to the amount of time the child spends with each parent regardless of who may have custody. However, the term "visitation" remains in common use.

If you have legal/full custody, you are the primary and final decision maker for significant matters regarding your children, such as which school they attend, who their health care providers are, and what church they will attend. The custodial parent is obligated to keep the noncustodial parent involved and should inform her or him when decisions have been made regarding the children. Ideally, the custodial parent will seek the opinion of the noncustodial parent before he or she makes any decisions involving the child.

Joint legal custody means that you and your former spouse will share equally in the decision making for your child. If you and the other parent are unable to reach agreement, you may need to return to mediation. Or, if the differences are significant, you may need to go to court to get the joint custody plan terminated.

Joint legal custody is often encouraged if the following conditions exist:

- Effective and open communication between the parents concerning the child
- A strong desire on the part of both parents to co-parent together
- A history of active involvement of both parents in the child's life
- Similar parenting values held by both parents
- A willingness on the part of both parents to place the child's needs before their own
- Both parents' willingness to be flexible and compromising about making decisions concerning the child.

Many people mistakenly believe that joint custody means that the time share or visitation schedule is 50/50, but most often it is not. You could have a joint custody plan where the children spend the overwhelming majority of their time with one parent. The time share plan can be whatever schedule that both parents agree upon.

8.2   On what basis will the judge award custody?

The judge considers many factors in determining child custody. The most important is "the best interest of the child." The following are some important factors a judge considers.

Stability. Does one parent change jobs a lot? Does one parent have an extended family near her or him? Has one parent throughout the marriage done more of the parenting? Is one parent more likely to keep the child on a routine? Which parent will make sure a child will get to all of her music lessons? Has Dad moved three times during the divorce process? Will Mom make sure the child gets her homework done each night?

Cooperation with the other parent. The court may consider your ability and willingness to be cooperative with the other parent. The court may also consider each parent's history of cooperation. The judge will consider who will make sure the time share (visitation) exchanges occur as scheduled and who will show flexibility with the schedule if it benefits the children.

Moral fitness. Does either parent have problems with alcohol, illicit drug abuse, prescription drug abuse, gambling, or committing crimes? With the prevalence of casinos now all over the state, gambling addiction has become a much more common problem in Oklahoma.

Age of the child. Oklahoma no longer ascribes to the "tender years" doctrine, which formerly gave a preference for custody of very young children to the mother. Despite this, if a child is very young and, for example, is breast-feeding, the mother has an advantage. When a child turns twelve he or she may express a preference as to which parent they would like to live with. Their preference does not decide the matter, but is simply another factor to be considered by the judge.

Mental health issues of the parents. Does one of the parents have issues with depression? Is one of the parents bipolar or schizophrenic? If so, it may have some impact on the judge's decision.

Capacity to provide physical care and satisfy educational needs. Here, the court may examine whether you or the other parent is better able to provide for your child's daily needs involving nutrition, health care, hygiene, social activities, and education. Which parent was the primary caregiver during the course of the marriage? Who attends the parent-teacher conferences? Who helps the children with homework? How are their grades?

Selflessness and dedication. Does one parent put the child's needs above their own? Does one parent have their act together more than the other parent and will follow an established routine with the child?

8.3   How can I make sure I will get to keep the children during the divorce proceedings?

A temporary court order is the best way to be sure your children will stay with you while your divorce is proceeding. Even if you and your spouse have agreed to temporary arrangements, talk with your attorney about whether this agreement should be formalized in a court order so that it can be enforced.

Obtaining a temporary order can be an important protection not only for the custody of your children, but for other issues such as support and temporary exclusive possession of the marital home.

Until a temporary order is entered, it's best that you continue to reside with your children if obtaining custody of them is important to you. It is usually recommended that the children stay in the family home. If you must leave your home, take your children with you and talk with your attorney about seeking the appropriate court orders. These might include orders for temporary protection, custody, support, possession of your home, or attorney fees.

8.4   How much weight does the child's preference carry?

The preference of your child is only one of many factors a judge considers in determining custody. A child does not get to pick which parent he or she will live with. As mentioned, a child must be at least twelve years old in Oklahoma in order to express a preference. However, if one child is twelve or older and another child is nine, the court may still interview both children, but in theory it is only the older child's preference that is supposed to matter. The practical reality is that the judge cannot forget what the nine-year-old says. Be careful not to coach your children if they are going to talk to the judge. All judges will look for this when they interview the child.

Judges can usually discern what a child really means, such as if a fourteen-year-old girl tells a judge that she wants to live with Mom because Dad is "mean and tries to control my life," and "Mom doesn't do that." What the judge hears is that Dad imposes discipline and Mom lets the girl do what she wants. The judge will prefer Dad's approach.

8.5   How can I prove that I was the primary care provider?

One tool to assist you and your attorney in establishing your case as a primary care provider is a Parental Roles Chart (see sample chart) indicating the care you and your spouse have each provided for your child. The clearer you are about the history of parenting, the better job your attorney can do in presenting your case to the judge.

It is understandable that if Mom has been the breadwinner and Dad stayed at home with the kids, he has an advantage, but the court understands that after the divorce this situation is likely to change. So don't despair if you have been the one who was the breadwinner.

Parental Roles Chart

Activity	Parent 1	Parent 2
Got up with child for feedings		
Got up with child when sick at night		
Bathed child		
Put child to sleep		
Potty-trained child		
Prepared and fed meals to child		
Helped child learn numbers, letters, colors		
Helped child learn to read		
Helped child with practice for sports, dance, music		
Took time off work for child's appointments		
Stayed home from work with sick child		
Took child to doctor visits		
Went to pharmacy for child's medication		
Administered child's medication		
Took child to therapy		
Took child to optometrist		

Parental Roles Chart (Continued)

Activity	Parent 1	Parent 2
Took child to dentist		
Took child to get haircuts		
Bought clothing for child		
Bought school supplies for child		
Transported child to school		
Picked child up after school		
Drove carpool for child's school		
Went to child's school activities		
Helped child with homework and projects		
Attended parent–teacher conferences		
Helped in child's classroom		
Chaperoned child's school trips and activities		
Transported child to day care		
Transported child from day care		
Attended day care activities		
Signed child up for sports, dance, music		
Bought equipment for sports, dance, music		
Transported child to sports, dance, music		
Attended child's sports, dance, music practices		
Attended child's sports, dance, music recitals		
Coached child's sports		
Transported child from sports, dance, music		
Knows child's friends and friends' families		
Took child to religious education		
Participated in child's religious education		
Obtained information and training about special needs of child		
Comforted child during times of emotional upset		

8.6 Do I have to let my spouse see the children before we are actually divorced?

Yes, unless your children are at risk for being harmed by your spouse or those living with your spouse, your children should maintain regular contact with the other parent. If their safety is at issue you may want to file pleadings asking the court to suspend visitation, but you need to be able to support your allegations.

It is important for children to experience the presence of both parents in their lives, regardless of the separation of the parents. Even if there is no temporary order for parenting time, cooperate with your spouse in making reasonable arrangements for time with your children.

8.7 I am seeing a therapist. Will that hurt my chances of getting custody?

This can be a question of degree. Mild depression is probably irrelevant; however, if you suffer from schizophrenia, it creates a much higher obstacle to overcome. Your well-being is important to your ability to be the best parent you can be. It may be that the condition for which you are being treated in no way affects your child or your ability to be a loving and supportive parent.

Your mental health records may be subpoenaed by the other parent's lawyer. For this reason, it is important to discuss with your attorney an action plan for responding to a request to obtain records in your therapist's file.

8.8 Can having a live-in partner hurt my chances of getting custody?

You can be sure that it will not help your case and it is more a question of how much can it hurt your chances of getting custody. If you are already living with your partner, let your attorney know right away so that the potential impact on any custody ruling can be assessed.

Your living with someone who is not your spouse may have significant impact on your custody case. However, judges' opinions of the significance of this factor can vary greatly. Talk promptly and frankly with your lawyer. It will be important that you look together at many aspects, including the following:

81

- How the judge assigned to your case views this situation
- Whether your living arrangement is likely to prompt a custody dispute that would otherwise not arise
- How long you have been separated from the other parent
- How long you have been in a relationship with your new partner
- The history and nature of the children's relationship with your partner
- Your future plans with your partner (such as marriage)

Living with a partner may put your custody case at risk. Consider such a decision thoughtfully, taking into account the advice of your lawyer.

8.9 Will all the sordid details of my or my spouse's affair have to come out in court in front of our children?

Judges make every effort to protect children from the conflict of their parents. The judges will not allow children to be present in the courtroom to hear the testimony of other witnesses. If one party wants the judge to talk to the children, all responsible judges will do this in their chambers outside of the parent's presence.

A bigger concern is your spouse or a family member telling your child what was said in the courtroom. You can request an instruction from the court ordering the parents to not discuss any of the testimony with the children. Nearly all judges will make this ruling.

8.10 Should I hire a private investigator to prove my spouse is having an affair?

It depends, but generally the expense does not justify the results. If custody is disputed and your spouse is having an affair, discuss with your attorney how a private investigator might help you gather evidence to support your case. Discuss the following considerations with your attorney:

- What view on extramarital relationships does my judge hold?

- How is the affair affecting the children?
- How much will a private investigator cost?
- What is the likelihood an investigator will provide evidence you can use?
- Will the evidence gathered help my case?

8.11 Will the fact that I had an affair during the marriage hurt my chances of getting custody?

Whether a past affair will have any impact on your custody case will depend upon many factors, including:

- The views of the judge assigned to your case
- Whether the affair had any impact on the children
- How long ago the affair occurred

Make sure you disclose this information to your attorney, even if the affair was ten years ago. When in doubt, tell your attorney everything.

8.12 During the months it takes to get a divorce, is it okay to date or will it hurt my chances at custody?

Dating during the divorce process is not a good idea. Your dating may be irrelevant if the children are unaware of it, but most judges will frown upon exposing your children to a new relationship when they are still adjusting to the separation of their parents. If your spouse is contesting custody, it would be best to focus your energy on your children, the litigation, and taking care of yourself.

If you do date and become sexually involved with your new partner, it is imperative that your children not be exposed to any sexual activity. If they are, it will harm your case. This includes having your new partner spend overnights when the children are present.

8.13 I'm gay and came out to my spouse when I filed for divorce. What impact will my sexual orientation have on my case for custody or parenting time?

Social science research shows that gay and lesbian parents are more similar than dissimilar to heterosexual parents. But you will likely need to address this issue because Oklahoma is the buckle of the Bible Belt, so it is quite possible it could have an adverse impact, depending on your judge. This attitude will change over time, but if you are reading this book in 2017 it will be quite a different matter than if you are reading it in 2026.

8.14 Can I have witnesses speak on my behalf as I try to get custody of my children?

Yes. At a trial for the final determination of custody, you and the other parent will each have an opportunity to have witnesses give live testimony. Affidavits from witnesses cannot be used. Among those you might consider as potential witnesses in your custody case are:

- Family members
- Friends
- Child-care providers
- Neighbors
- Teachers
- Counselors
- Health care providers

In deciding which witnesses would best support your case, your attorney may consider the following:

- What has been this witness's opportunity to observe you or the other parent, especially with your child. How frequently? How recently?
- How long has the witness known you or the other parent?
- What is the relationship of the witness to the child and the parents?
- How valuable is the knowledge that this witness has?
- Does this witness have knowledge different from that of other witnesses?
- Is the witness available and willing to testify?
- Is the witness clear in conveying information?
- Is the witness credible, that is, will the judge believe this witness?
- Does the witness have any bias or prejudice that could impact the testimony? For example, your mom would be a biased witness.

Support your attorney by providing a list of potential witnesses together with your opinion regarding the answers to the previous questions. Give your attorney the phone numbers, addresses, and occupations of each of your potential witnesses. When parents give conflicting testimony during a custody trial, the testimony of other witnesses can be key to determining the outcome of the case.

8.15 Can the children speak to the judge?

If either you or your spouse wants to have the judge listen to what your child has to say (See question 8.4 above), a request is ordinarily made to the judge to have the child speak to the judge in the judge's office (chambers) rather than from the witness stand. I have, unfortunately, seen at least one judge allow an older child to be questioned in open court by the attorneys and in front of the parents. Thankfully, this is the rare exception.

Most judges will allow attorneys to submit questions for the judge to ask the children in the judge's office, but typically the attorneys will not be able to directly question the children. If you have concerns about the other parent learning what your child says to the judge, talk to your lawyer about the possibility of obtaining a court order keeping this information from both parents.

Typically, the testimony of the child is made "on the record" (in the presence of a court reporter). This is so that the testimony can be transcribed later in the event of an appeal.

8.16 Will my attorney want to speak with my children?

In most cases your attorney won't ask to speak with your children. An exception might be where custody is disputed or where either parent has made allegations of abuse or neglect.

Not all attorneys are trained in appropriate interviewing techniques for children, especially for younger children. If the attorney has not spent a lot of time with children or is not familiar with child development, the interview may not provide meaningful information. Don't hesitate to ask your attorney about his or her experience in working with children before you agree to an interview of your child.

If your attorney asks to meet with your child, provide some background information about your child first. Let your attorney know about your child's personality, some of his or her interests, and any topics that might upset your child. This background will help the attorney exercise the care essential anytime a professional questions a child.

8.17   What is a *guardian ad litem?* Why is one appointed?

The *guardian ad litem (GAL)* is an attorney or mental health professional appointed by the court to investigate all matters impacting the best interest of the children and will recommend what he or she believes is in the child or children's best interest. Most often they are appointed in cases where there is high conflict or someone has been accused of abusing a child.

The guardian *ad litem* may be called as a witness by you or your spouse to give testimony of her or his knowledge, based upon their investigation. The guardian *ad litem* can oftentimes introduce information that the judge might not otherwise hear. In some cases, the attorneys may agree that a written report prepared by the guardian *ad litem* be received into evidence for the judge's consideration. Typically, the recommendations of the guardian *ad litem* have a great deal of impact on what the judge decides about custody and visitation of children.

8.18   Why might I not be awarded custody?

You will not be awarded custody if the judge determines that you are not fit to be a custodial parent. You may also not be awarded custody in the event the judge determines that, although you are fit to be awarded custody, it is in your child's best interest that custody is awarded to the other parent. A decision by the judge that your spouse should have custody does not require a conclusion that you are an unfit parent.

Determinations of your fitness to be a custodial parent and of the best interest of your child will largely depend upon the facts of your case. Reasons why a parent might be found to be unfit include a history of physical abuse, alcohol or drug abuse, or mental health problems that affect the ability to parent. The judge could determine that one parent consistently speaks ill of the other parent in front of the children or refuses to puts his or her personal needs ahead of those of the children. A judge's ruling on the best interest of a child is based upon numerous factors (see also question 8.2).

8.19 Does joint custody always mean equal time at each parent's house?

No. Joint custody does not necessarily mean an equal division of parenting time/visitation, nor does it require that the child flip-flop every other week between two homes.

Whether it is sole or joint custody, you and your spouse can agree to share parenting time/visitation in a way that best serves your children. An example would be: You and your spouse agree to joint legal custody, but you will have physical custody, meaning your child will live with you. It can also be helpful to remember that day-to-day decisions, such as a child's daily routine, will usually be made by the parent who has the child that day.

8.20 What are some of the risks of joint custody?

Joint custody may be a good idea when the parents agree to it and they have been separated for a period of time and have been able to reach decisions regarding their children without the involvement of attorneys or the court. However, many factors can arise after the divorce, even if you and your ex-spouse have a great relationship. If you or your former spouse remarries, a new spouse can negatively impact the joint custody plan. Joint custody requires healthy communication between you and your ex-spouse. Without it, you are at risk for conflict, stress, and delay when making important decisions for your child. If communication with your ex-spouse regarding your child is poor, joint custody is probably not a good option.

8.21 If my spouse is awarded physical custody, how much time will our child spend with me?

Parenting time/visitation schedules for noncustodial parents vary from case to case. As in the determination of custody, the best interest of the child is what a court considers in determining the parenting time schedule. Among the factors that can impact a parenting time schedule are the past history of parenting time, the age and needs of the child, the parents' work schedules, and the distance between the parents' homes.

If you and your spouse are willing to reach your own agreement about the parenting time schedule, you are likely to be more satisfied with it than with one imposed by a judge.

If you and your spouse are unable to reach an agreement on a shared time/visitation schedule, either on your own or with the assistance of your lawyers or a mediator, the judge will decide the schedule.

8.22 What is a *shared time* or *standard minimum noncustodial visitation schedule*?

A *shared time* or *standard minimum noncustodial visitation schedule* is a document that details the amount of time you and your spouse will have with the children after the divorce is finalized. Among the issues addressed in the standard minimum noncustodial visitation schedule are:

- Parenting time, including specific times for:
    - Regular school year
    - Holidays
    - Birthdays
    - Mother's Day and Father's Day
    - Summer
    - School breaks
- Phone access to the child
- Communication regarding the child
- Access to records regarding the child
- Notice regarding parenting time
- Attendance at the child's activities
- Exchange of information such as addresses, phone numbers, and care providers

See the Sample Standard Minimum Noncustodial Visitation Schedule in the Appendix.

8.23 I don't think it's safe for my children to have any contact with my spouse. How can I prove this to the judge?

Arrest records, testimony from a counselor or therapist, and Department of Human Services (DHS) findings of abuse all are tools that can be utilized to suspend visitation. You may need a protection order, supervised visitation, or certain restrictions on your spouse's parenting time. Your attorney also needs information about your spouse, such as whether your spouse is or has been:

- Using alcohol or drugs
- Treated for alcohol or drug use
- Arrested, charged, or convicted of crimes of violence
- In possession of firearms
- Subject to a protection order for harassment or violence

Keep in mind, if you had a ten-year marriage you are going to be asked by the other lawyer why it was safe for your spouse to raise the children for ten years, but now that you are divorcing it is suddenly unsafe for the children?

Even "bad parents" will be given opportunities to see their children on a progressively increasing schedule if they follow the guidelines the court sets for them.

8.24 My spouse keeps saying he'll get custody because there were no witnesses to his abuse and I can't prove it. Is he right?

No. Most domestic violence is not witnessed by others, and judges know this.

If you have been a victim of abusive behavior by your spouse, or if you have witnessed your children as victims, your testimony is likely to be the most compelling evidence. See the discussion of abuse in chapter 7.

Be sure to tell your attorney about anyone who may have either seen your spouse's behavior or spoken to you or your children right after an abusive incident. They may be important witnesses in your custody case.

8.25 I am concerned about protecting my child from abuse by my spouse. Which types of past abuse by my spouse are important to tell my attorney?

Keeping your child safe is your top priority. So that your attorney can help you protect your child, give him or her a full history of the following:

- Hitting, kicking, pushing, shoving, or slapping you or your child
- Sexual abuse
- Threats of harm to you or the child
- Threats to abduct your child
- Destruction of property
- Torture or other harm to pets
- Requiring your child to keep secrets

The process of writing down past events may help you to remember other incidents of abuse that you had forgotten. Be as complete as possible.

8.26 How can I get the other parent's visitation to be supervised?

It may be that a protective order is warranted to terminate or limit contact with your children. You will need to show that harm to the children is caused by the spouse/parent or some other person or situation under her or his control.

Ask your attorney whether, under the facts of your case, the judge would consider any of the following court orders:

- Supervised visits
- Visitation with the children in a public place
- Parenting class for the other parent
- Anger management or other rehabilitative program for the other parent
- A prohibition against drinking by the other parent when with the children

Judges have differing approaches to cases when children are at risk. Recognize that there are also often practical considerations, such as cost or the availability of people to supervise visits. If this is conduct that occurred throughout the marriage and you are just now bringing it up, you will need to explain why was it allowed during the marriage.

8.27 I want to talk to my spouse about our child, but all she wants to do is argue. How can I communicate without it always turning into a fight?

Because conflict is high between you and your spouse, consider the following:

- Ask your lawyer to help you obtain a court order for custody and parenting time that is specific and detailed. This lowers the amount of necessary communication between you and your spouse.
- Put as much information in writing as possible.
- Avoid criticisms of your spouse's parenting or directing their parenting.
- Find a mutual friend or family member you both respect to be present.
- Be factual, concise, and business-like.
- Acknowledge to your spouse the good parental qualities he or she displays, such as being concerned, attentive, or generous.
- Keep your child out of any conflicts.

8.28 What if our child is not returned from parenting time at the agreed-upon time? Should I call the police?

Calling the police should be done only as a last resort if you feel that your child is at risk for abuse or neglect, or if you have been advised by your attorney that such a call is warranted. The involvement of law enforcement officials in parental conflict can result in far greater trauma to a child than a late return at the end of a parenting time.

The appropriate response to a child not being returned according to a court order depends upon the circumstances. *Contempt* may be one option, but make sure you document in writing (this can be by letter or e-mail, preferably not by text, which is not as easy to show in court) to your spouse that they were late. Neither calling them nor confronting them at the exchange where children are present is a good idea. Verbal communication whether in person or on the phone becomes a he-said-she-said proof problem in court.

8.29   If I have full custody, may I move out of state without the permission of the court?

No. A custodial parent must obtain permission of the court prior to moving out of state with a child. You must notify your ex-spouse in writing of your intention to move. If your former spouse agrees to your move, contact your attorney for preparing and submitting the necessary documents to your former spouse and the court for approval.

If your former spouse objects to your move, you must apply to the court for permission, give your spouse notice of the application, and have a court hearing for the judge to decide. Oklahoma has a *Relocation Act* that must be complied with.

To obtain the court's permission, you must first prove that you have a legitimate reason for the move, such as a better job or a transfer of your new spouse's employment. You must also prove that the move benefits the child and not just you.

8.30   What factors does the court consider when determining the best interest of the child regarding a move?

In determining your child's best interest, the court may consider many factors. These can include your child's ties to Oklahoma and family here, the quality of the community you want to move to, and how often your spouse would see the child. If you're considering an out-of-state move, talk to your attorney immediately. There are important facts for you to gather as soon as possible about potential housing, school, and day care.

8.31   After the divorce, can my spouse legally take our children out of the state during their visitation? Out of the country?

Most court orders do not address this issue, therefore yes they can. If you are concerned about your children being taken out of Oklahoma by the other parent, discuss the possibility of some of these decree provisions regarding out-of-state travel with your child:

- Limits on the duration or distance for out-of-state travel with the child
- Notice requirements
- Information on phone numbers
- Information on physical addresses
- E-mail address contact information
- Possession of the child's passport with the court
- Posting of bond by the other parent prior to travel
- Requiring a court order for travel outside the country

Although judges are not ordinarily concerned about short trips across state lines, you should let your attorney know if you are concerned that your child may be abducted by the other parent so that reasonable safeguards may be put in place.

8.32 If I am not given custody, what rights do I have regarding medical records and school records for my child?

Regardless of which parent has custody, state law allows both parents to have access to the medical records and school records of their children. Communicate with the other parent to both share and receive information about your child's progress in school and extracurricular activities. This will enable you to support your child and each other through any challenging periods of your child's education. Regardless of which parent has custody, your child will benefit from both parents' involvement in his or her education and by their participation in parent-teacher conferences, attendance at school events, and help with school homework.

8.33 What if my child does not want to go for his or her parenting time? Can my former spouse force the child to go?

If your child is resisting going with the other parent, it can first be helpful to determine the underlying reason. Consider these questions:

- What is your child's stated reason for not wanting to go?
- Does your child appear afraid, anxious, or sad?
- Do you have any concerns regarding your child's safety while with the other parent?
- Have you prepared your child for being with the other parent, speaking about the experience with enthusiasm and encouragement?
- Is it possible your child is perceiving your anxiety about the situation and is consequently having the same reaction?
- Have you spoken to the other parent about your child's behavior?
- Can you provide anything that will make your child's time with the other parent more comfortable, such as a favorite toy or blanket?
- Have you established clear routines that support your child to be ready to go with the other parent with ease, such as packing a backpack or saying good-bye to a family pet?

If you suspect that your spouse is attempting to alienate your children from you, discuss the topic of parental alienation with your attorney. Generally speaking, until the children reach the age of about fifteen, it is the duty of the parent to take the children to the visitation whether the children want to go or not. Courts expect the time share or visitation to be followed. If your spouse is consistently not doing this, talk to your attorney about filing contempt or a motion to enforce visitation.

8.34 What steps can I take to prevent my spouse from getting the children in the event of my death?

Legally, in the event of your death, the children would automatically go to the other parent. You can state a preference in your will, but that will not overcome the legal presumption that the other parent is the next person in line for custody. This does not prevent your mother or father or anyone from filing their own guardianship action for custody of the children.

9

Child Support

Whether you will be paying child support or receiving it, it is often the subject of much worry. Will I receive enough support to take care of my children? Will I have enough money to live on after I pay my child support? How will I make ends meet?

Most parents want to provide for their children. Today, the child-support laws make it possible for parents to have a better understanding of their obligation to support their children. The mechanisms for both payment and receipt of child support are more clearly defined, and help is available for collecting support if it's not paid.

The Oklahoma Department of Human Services Child Support Guidelines and the Child Support Enforcement Office are designed to make the child-support process less complex. Although the process can be confusing, matters that appear complex in the beginning will eventually become routine for you and the other parent.

9.1　What determines whether I will get child support?

Whether you will receive child support depends upon a number of factors. These may include the number of overnights that your child is living in your household versus that of your spouse, and the respective incomes of you and your spouse. When one spouse is self-employed this almost always creates a dispute over how much income should go toward child custody.

If you have physical custody of your child, it is likely your spouse will be ordered to pay support for any children born or adopted during your marriage.

9.2 Can I request child support even if I do not meet the six-month residency requirement?

Yes. Even though you may not meet the residency requirement to obtain a divorce, you have a right to seek support for your children. Go to your local office of Department of Human Services or go to www.okdhs.org/services/ocss/Pages/default.aspx.

9.3 Can I get temporary support while waiting for custody to be decided?

Yes. A judge has authority to enter a temporary order for custody and child support. This order ordinarily remains in place until a final decree establishing custody is entered. In most cases a hearing for temporary custody and support can be held shortly after the filing of the petition for divorce.

9.4 What is *temporary support* and how soon can I get it?

Temporary support is paid for the support of a spouse or a child. It is paid sometime after the divorce petition is filed and continues until your final decree of divorce is entered by the court or a new court order is entered.

If you are in need of temporary support, talk to your attorney at your first opportunity. If an agreement with your spouse cannot be reached, it is likely that your attorney will file a motion for temporary support asking the judge to decide how much the support should be and when it will start.

The following are the common steps in the process:

- Your lawyer requests a hearing date from the judge and prepares the necessary documents.
- A temporary hearing is held.
- The temporary order is signed by the judge.
- Your spouse's employer is notified to begin withholding your support from your spouse's paychecks.

- Your spouse's employer sends the support through Oklahoma Child Support in Oklahoma City and you will receive the money through a credit card.

If your spouse is not paying you support voluntarily, time is of the essence in obtaining a temporary order for support, so discuss this with your attorney as soon as possible.

9.5 How soon does my spouse have to start paying support for the children?

Your spouse may begin paying you support voluntarily at any time. A temporary order for support will give you the right to collect the support if your spouse stops paying. Talk to your lawyer about court hearings for temporary support in your county. You may have to wait for two or three weeks before your temporary hearing can be held. It is possible that the judge will not order child support to start until the first of the following month.

9.6 How is the amount of child support I'll receive or pay figured?

The Oklahoma Child Support Guidelines provide that both parents have a duty to contribute to the support of their children in proportion to their respective incomes. As a result, both your income and the income of your spouse will factor into the child-support calculation.

Other factors the court may consider include:

- The additional cost of health insurance for the child
- Regularly paid support for other children
- Substantial fluctuations of annual earnings by either parent during the immediate past three years
- The number of overnights the child spends with each parent

It is rare, but a judge may order an amount of support that is different from the guidelines amount. This is referred to as a deviation and may be a higher or lower amount. Child support that is higher or lower than what the guidelines provide for may be awarded in certain cases, for example:

- When either parent or child has extraordinary medical costs

- When a child is disabled with special needs
- For juveniles placed in foster care
- Whenever the application of the guidelines in an individual case would be unjust or inappropriate

Due to the complexity of calculations under the guidelines, many attorneys use computer software to calculate child support. You can review the calculator in greater detail at www.okdhs.org/onlineservices/cscalc/Pages/cscalc.aspx.

9.7   Will the type of custody arrangement or the amount of parenting time I have impact the amount of child support I receive?

Generally, no. Primarily it comes down to the number of overnights that each parent has and their incomes. A dispute may occur over how many overnights a parent is supposed to have according to the court order in comparison to the actual number.

9.8   Is overtime pay considered in the calculation of child support?

Yes, if your overtime is a regular part of your employment and you can actually expect to earn it regularly. The court will likely look at whether you received overtime during the last two to three years.

9.9   Will rental income be factored into my child support, or just my salary?

Yes. Income from almost any source is going to be considered. However, if your spouse remarries, the new spouse's income is not considered as income to your former spouse.

9.10   My spouse has a college degree, but refuses to get a job. Will the court consider this in determining the amount of child support?

The earning capacity of your spouse may be considered instead of their current income. The court can look at your spouse's work history, education, skills, health, and job opportunities and conclude that your spouse is capable of earning more than he or she is actually making.

9.11   Will I get the child support directly from my spouse or from the state?

The majority of people receiving child support today receive it from the Oklahoma Department of Human Services Child Support Services. If the children are on SoonerCare (Oklahoma Medicaid), the child support will come from DHS Child Support Services.

9.12   If my spouse sends in a child-support payment to the state, how quickly will I receive it?

A number of factors affect how quickly your child-support payment will be paid to you after it is received by the DHS in Oklahoma City, but typically it will be deposited in your credit card account within two days after it is received by DHS. Only the state DHS can deposit money into this credit card account.

9.13   Is there any reason not to pay or receive payments directly to or from my spouse once the court has entered a child-support order?

Yes. The DHS Child Support Enforcement Office can act as an official calculator of how much support has been paid and how much is owed. If you move to a different address or city, or if you lose records, a dispute may arise over how much has been paid.

If your ex-spouse owes you back child support and the amount owed is high enough, DHS can take action by doing one or all of the following: filing a contempt citation against the delinquent spouse, intercepting the spouse's tax return, and suspending their driver's license. A private attorney can file a contempt action for failure to pay child support sooner than the state can act; however, the state has more enforcement tools at their disposal, so it is a good idea to go through the state.

9.14   How soon can I expect my child-support payments to start arriving?

A number of factors impact this answer. The first is how quickly the lawyers get a finalized order to DHS Child Support Services, but it certainly should be done within sixty days of the order being sent to DHS. Remember that you are going through a government agency and they have policies and procedures that must be followed.

9.15 Will some amount of child support be withheld from every paycheck?

It depends upon the employer's policy and how you are paid. If support is due on the first of the month, the employer has the full month to withhold the amount ordered to be paid. If an employer issues checks every other week, which is twenty-six pay periods per year, there will be some months in which a third paycheck is issued. Over time, child-support payments typically fall into a routine schedule, which makes it easier for both the payor and the recipient of support to plan their budgets.

9.16 If my spouse has income other than from an employer, is it still possible to get a court order to withhold my child support from his income?

Yes. Child support can be automatically withheld from most sources of income. These may include unemployment, worker's compensation, retirement plans, and investment income.

9.17 The person I am divorcing is not the biological parent of my child. Can I still collect child support from my spouse?

Perhaps. Your spouse may be ordered to pay child support under certain circumstances. If, for example, the child was born during the marriage and the marriage lasted at least two years, your spouse legally becomes the father of that child.

9.18 Can I collect child support from both the biological parent and the adoptive parent of my child?

When your child was adopted, the biological parent's duty to support your child ended. However, it may be possible for you to collect past-due child support from the period of time before the adoption.

9.19 What happens with child support when our children go to other parent's home for summer vacation? Is child support still due?

Generally, yes. In most cases when child support is set up, it is calculated for a year period with the total number of overnights for each year for each parent being calculated; this factors in holidays and summer visitation. The parent paying the support may get a reduction in the support if she or he has more than 121 overnights per year.

9.20 After the divorce, if I choose to live with my new partner rather than marry, can I still collect child support?

Yes. Although spousal support (alimony) may end if you live with your partner, child support does not terminate for this reason.

9.21 Can I still collect child support if I move to another state?

Yes. A move out of state will not end your right to receive child support.

9.22 Can I expect to continue to receive child support if I remarry?

Yes. Your child support will continue even if you remarry.

9.23 How long can I expect to receive child support?

Under Oklahoma law, child support is ordinarily ordered to be paid until the child turns eighteen. However, if the child has not graduated and is still attending high school, the support does not end until the child turns twenty years old.

9.24 Does interest accrue on past-due child support?

Yes, interest accrues on past-due child support. The current rate is 2 percent.

9.25 What can I do if my former spouse refuses to pay child support?

If your former spouse is not paying child support, you may take action to enforce the court order either with the help of your lawyer or the assistance of child-support services the through DHS Child Support Services. For the Oklahoma City metropolitan area call (405) 522-2273, Tulsa metro area (918) 295-3500, all other areas call (800) 522-2922 or you may go to their website at www.okdhs.org/services/ocss/Pages/default. aspx.

The judge may order payment of both the current amount of support and an additional amount to be paid each month until the past-due child support (referred to as arrearages) is paid in full.

DHS Child Support Services may intercept your spouse's state or federal income tax refund and direct that money to you. It may also be possible to garnish a checking or savings account. A driver's license may also be suspended if a parent falls behind in child-support payments. However, if there is a payment plan for the payment of arrearages, the driver's license will not be suspended.

Your former spouse may also be found in contempt of court if the failure to pay support is intentional. Possible consequences include being fined or jailed. A private attorney will take action sooner than DHS Child Support Services. If your spouse is found in contempt, he or she may be required to pay your attorney fee.

9.26 At what point will the state help me collect back child support, and what methods do they use?

It depends. When the state will help you collect back child support and the methods they will use can depend upon the amount of back child support owed.

A driver's license and recreational and professional licenses can be suspended depending on the number of payments missed and the amount owed. You must initiate contact with the DHS Child Support Services if you cannot afford a private attorney.

9.27 I live outside Oklahoma. Will the money I spend on airline tickets to see my children impact my child support?

It might. If you expect to spend large sums of money for transportation in order to have parenting time with your children, talk to your attorney about how this might be taken into consideration when determining child-support payments.

9.28 After the divorce, can my former spouse substitute buying sprees with the child for child-support payments?

No. Purchases of gifts and clothing for a child do not relieve your former spouse from an obligation to pay you child support.

9.29 Are expenses such as child care supposed to be taken out of my child support?

No. Child-care expenses are separate from child support because the Oklahoma Child Support Guidelines recognize that child care for young children is often a considerable expense. Your child-support guideline percentage that is calculated on the child-support computation form will also be the same percentage you are expected to pay for day care in addition to the child-support amount.

9.30 Can my spouse be required by the decree to pay for our child's private elementary and high school education?

Not unless the parties voluntarily entered into this agreement at the time the divorce decree was entered and it is part of the decree. Otherwise, the judge will not order this. The spouse paying child support may get a credit on the monthly child support if he or she is paying all of the private school tuition for the children.

9.31 Can my spouse be required by the decree to contribute financially to our child's college education?

No. But if your spouse voluntarily agreed to do this and it is part of the divorce decree the judge will enforce this provision if a contempt action is filed.

10

Alimony

The mere mention of the word "alimony" might stir your emotions and start your stomach churning. If your spouse filed for divorce and sought alimony, you might see it as is a double injustice—your marriage is ending and you feel like you have to pay for it, too. If you are seeking alimony, you might feel hurt and confused that your spouse is resistant to helping to support you, even though you interrupted your career to stay home and care for your children.

Learning more about Oklahoma's laws on alimony, also referred to as spousal support, can help you move from your emotional reaction to it to the reality of possible outcomes in your case. Uncertainty about the precise amount of alimony that may be awarded or the number of years it might be paid is not unusual. Work closely with your lawyer. Try looking at it from your spouse's perspective.

With the help of your lawyer, you will know the best course of action to take toward an alimony decision you can live with after your divorce is over.

10.1 Which gets calculated first, child support or alimony?

Child support. Spousal support is not directly related to child support. It is, however, a factor the court will look at to determine the ability the higher-income spouse has to pay their soon-to-be ex-spouse.

10.2 What's the difference between *spousal support* and *alimony?*

In Oklahoma, the terms "alimony" and "spousal support" mean the same thing.

10.3 Are there different types of alimony?

Yes, there are two types. The first type of alimony that most people think of is what Oklahoma calls *support alimony;* this is designed to offset the loss in the standard of living that the lower-income spouse will have as a result of the divorce.

The second type of alimony is known as *property division alimony.* Property division alimony typically is not associated with need, but on other factors in the marriage. For example, property division alimony may be awarded in a case in which one spouse worked diligently to contribute to the overall marital property while the other spouse gambled away money and had substance abuse problems. Under these circumstances, a court might award the diligent spouse property division alimony to make the overall division of the marital property more fair. In other words, the spouse who had worked so diligently would be awarded more property.

10.4 How will I know if I am eligible to receive alimony?

Judges vary greatly in their opinions about whether to award alimony. One judge might award alimony where another would not. Talk with your attorney about whether you are a candidate for alimony. Among the factors that may affect your eligibility to receive alimony are:

- The length of your marriage
- Your contributions to the marriage, including the interruption of your career for the care of children or to support your spouse's career
- Your education, work history, health, income, and earning capacity
- Your overall financial situation compared to that of your spouse
- Your need for support
- Your spouse's ability to pay support

Every case for alimony is unique. Providing your lawyer with clear and detailed information about the facts of your marriage and current situation will increase the likelihood of a fair outcome for you.

10.5 What information should I provide to my attorney if I want alimony?

If your attorney advises you that you may be a candidate for alimony, be sure to provide complete facts about your situation, including:

- A history of the interruptions in your education or career for the benefit of your spouse, including transfers or moves due to your spouse's employment
- A history of the interruptions in your education or career for raising children, including periods during which you worked part-time
- Your complete educational background, including the dates of your schooling or training and degrees earned
- Your work history, including the names of your employers, the dates of your employment, your duties, your pay, and the reason you left
- Any pensions or other benefits lost due to the interruption of your career for the benefit of the marriage
- Your health history, including any current diagnoses, treatments, limitations, and medications
- Your monthly living expenses, including anticipated future expenses such as health insurance and tax on alimony
- A complete list of the debts for you and your spouse
- Income for you and your spouse, including all sources

Mention any other factors that might affect your need for alimony. For example, your need for future medical treatment, a lack of jobs in the field in which you were formerly employed, or the fact that you stayed home and raised your children for many years. No two alimony cases are alike.

10.6 My spouse told me that because I had an affair during the marriage, I have no chance to get alimony even though I quit my job and have cared for our children for many years. Is it true that I have no case?

No. Your right to alimony will be based upon many factors, but having an affair is not an absolute bar to getting spousal support.

10.7 How is the amount of alimony calculated?

Unlike child support, there are not specific guidelines for determining the amount of alimony. A judge will look at the expenses and incomes of you and your spouse, after giving consideration to the payment and overall assets that you are receiving.

Judges are given a lot of discretion to make their own decision on alimony without the benefit of specific guidelines. Consequently, the outcome of an alimony ruling by a judge can be one of the most unpredictable aspects of your divorce.

10.8 My spouse makes a lot more money than he reports on our tax return, but he hides it. How can I prove my spouse's real income to show he can afford to pay alimony?

If your husband is self-employed this is always a problem. Judges assume that tax returns shows one's actual income. If you want to prove your spouse makes more money, you may have to hire an accountant or even a business evaluator. Your lawyer may have to engage in extensive discovery that will cost you more money, so weigh the costs carefully. The party requesting the alimony has the burden to prove the need for the alimony.

10.9 How is the purpose of alimony different from the payment of my property settlement?

Spousal support and the division of property serve two distinct purposes, even though many of the factors for determining them are the same. The purpose of alimony is to pay for your continued support, whereas the purpose of a property division is to distribute the marital assets fairly between you and your spouse.

10.10 How long can I expect to receive alimony?

The trend in Oklahoma has been to reduce the length of time alimony is paid. Alimony is meant to cover costs for "readjustment." The length of time you will receive alimony depends upon the facts of your case and the judge's philosophy toward alimony. In general, the longer your marriage, the stronger your case is for a long-term alimony award.

You may receive only temporary alimony, or you may receive alimony for several years. Talk to your attorney about the facts of your case to get a clearer picture of the possible outcomes in your situation. Unless you and your spouse agree otherwise, your alimony will terminate upon your remarriage or the death of either of you.

10.11 Does remarriage affect my alimony?

Yes. Alimony ends upon remarriage of the person receiving the alimony.

10.12 Can I continue to collect alimony if I move to a different state?

Yes. The duty of your former spouse to follow a court order to pay alimony does not end simply because you move to another state.

10.13 What can I do if my spouse stops paying alimony?

If your spouse stops paying alimony, see your attorney about filing a contempt action. In a contempt action your spouse may be ordered to appear in court and provide evidence, explaining why support has not been paid. Possible consequences for contempt of court include a jail sentence or a fine.

10.14 Can I return to court to modify alimony?

Yes. If there has been a material change in the financial status of either spouse, he or she may seek to have alimony modified. Examples include a serious illness or the loss or obtaining of a job. Alimony could be reduced if, for example, the spouse receiving the income now makes considerably more money than the former spouse at the time of the divorce.

11

Division of Property

You never imagined that you would face losing the house you and your spouse so happily moved into—the house where you celebrated family traditions and spent countless hours making it "home." Your spouse wants it and your lawyer says it might have to be sold.

During a divorce, you will decide whether you or your spouse will take ownership of everything from bathroom towels to the stock portfolio. Suddenly you find yourself having a strong attachment to that lamp in the family room or the painting in the hallway. Why does the collection of coins suddenly take on new meaning?

Do your best to reach agreement regarding dividing household goods. Enlist the support of your attorney in deciding which assets should be valued by an expert, such as the family business or real estate. From tax consequences to replacement value, there are many factors to consider in deciding whether to fight to keep an asset, to give it to your spouse, or to have it sold.

Like all aspects of your divorce, take one step at a time. By starting with the items most easily divided, you and your spouse can avoid paying lawyers to litigate the value of that 1980s album collection.

11.1 What system does Oklahoma use for dividing property?

Oklahoma law provides for an equitable or fair, but not necessarily equal, division of the property and debts acquired during your marriage.

Regardless of how title is held (whose name is on a property), the court can use its discretion to make a division of the marital assets. In many cases, as little as one-third of the assets awarded to one party and two-thirds to the other and may still be considered "equitable."

The court will consider a number of factors, including your debts, the circumstances of you and your spouse, and the history of contributions to the marriage.

11.2 What does *community property* mean?

In states having *community property* laws, each spouse holds a one-half interest in most property acquired during the marriage. Oklahoma is not a community property state, so community property law does not apply here.

11.3 How is it determined who gets the house?

The first issue regarding the family home is often a determination of who will retain possession of it while the divorce is pending. The entire division of assets and debts, as well as where the children will spend most of their time, must be evaluated in looking at who will be awarded the marital residence. If you and your spouse are unable to reach agreement regarding the house, the judge will decide who keeps it or whether it will be sold.

11.4 Should I sell the house during the divorce proceedings?

Marital property cannot be sold during the divorce unless both parties agree or the judge allows certain property to be sold in a temporary order.

11.5 What is meant by *equity* in my home?

Equity in the home is the amount of money that the house would sell for above what is owed on the mortgage. For example, if the first mortgage is $50,000 and the second mortgage from a home equity loan is $10,000, the total debt owed against the house is $60,000. If your home is valued at $100,000, the equity in your home is $40,000 (the $100,000 value less the $60,000 in mortgages equals $40,000 in equity).

If one of the parties keeps the home, the issue of how to give the other party his or her share of the equity must be considered.

11.6   How will the equity in our house be divided?

If your home is going to be sold, the equity in the home will most likely be divided at the time of the sale, after the costs of the sale have been paid.

If either you or your spouse will be awarded the house, there are a number of options for the other party being compensated for his or her share of the equity in the marital home. These could include:

- The spouse who does not receive the house receives other assets (for example, retirement funds) to compensate for the value of the equity.
- The person who remains in the home agrees to refinance the home at some future date and to pay the other party his or her share of the equity.
- The parties agree that the property be sold at a future date, or upon the happening of a certain event such as the youngest child completing high school or the remarriage of the party keeping the home.

As the residence is often among the most valuable assets considered in a divorce, the following factors should be discussed with your attorney:

- Valuation of the property
- Your ability to refinance the home solely in your name
- The dates on which certain actions should be taken, such as listing the home for sale
- The real estate agent's fee
- Mortgage payments

11.7   Who keeps all the household goods until the divorce decree is signed?

The court will ordinarily not make any decisions about who keeps the household goods on a temporary basis. If the couple cannot agree on how to divide the goods, the court will decide. If the court decides, it is usually a 50/50 split.

11.8 How are assets such as cars, boats, and furniture divided, and when does this happen?

In most cases spouses are able to reach their own agreements about how to divide personal property, such as household furnishings and vehicles.

If you and your spouse disagree about how to divide certain items, it can be wise to consider which are truly valuable to you, financially or otherwise. Perhaps some of them can be easily replaced. Always look to see whether it is a good use of your attorney fees to argue over items of personal property. If a negotiated settlement cannot be reached, the issue of the division of your property will be made by the judge at trial.

11.9 What is meant by a *division of assets proposal*?

A *division of assets proposal* is a list or chart of the property you and your spouse own regardless of whether it was acquired before marriage or not. It may also include a brief description of the property and the value you believe the property is worth. If you know the value your spouse places on the property, you would list that also.

The division of assets will become a trial exhibit showing how you propose the marital property should be divided. Generally, property owned prior to the marriage will be returned to that spouse who brought it into the marriage unless your spouse has done something to contribute to its value.

Typically, the division will assign each piece of property to one spouse. In most cases when the columns are added up the value of the property awarded to you should be roughly the same amount awarded to your spouse. Reasons why it might not be 50/50 would be if one spouse makes significantly more money than the other spouse or one spouse is receiving alimony.

11.10 How and when are liquid assets such as bank accounts and stocks divided?

When the divorce petition is filed, it will be served along with a document called an automatic temporary injunction that prevents either side from selling assets or hiding assets during the course of the divorce unless both sides agree to the sale.

While your divorce is in progress, discuss with your attorney whether you should keep an accounting of how you spend money and whether that money is in an individual bank account or a joint account. Stocks and large bank accounts are ordinarily part of the final agreement for the division of property and debts. If you and your spouse cannot agree on how your investments should be divided, a judge will make the decision at trial.

11.11 How is pet custody determined?

This is becoming a more frequent issue. Some judges believe that getting involved with these matters is beneath their dignity, so they may seem cranky regarding this issue. Nevertheless, they treat pets more as property division than anything else. Factors they might look at are:

- Who held title to the pet?
- Who provided care for the pet?
- Who will best be able to meet the pet's needs?

Some courts have awarded the pet to one party and given the other party certain rights, such as:

- Specific periods of time to be spent with the pet
- The right to care for the pet when the other person is not able to
- The right to be informed of the pet's health condition

11.12 How will our property in another state be divided?

For the purposes of dividing your assets, out-of-state property is treated the same as property in Oklahoma.

11.13 I worked hard for years to support my family while my spouse completed an advanced degree. Do I have a right to any of my spouse's future earnings?

Possibly. Your contributions during the marriage are a factor to be considered in both the division of the property and debts, as well as any award of alimony. Be sure to give your attorney a complete history of your contributions to the marriage and ask about their impact on the outcome of your case.

11.14 Are all of the assets—such as property, bank accounts, and inheritances—that I had prior to my marriage still going to be mine after the divorce?

It depends. In many cases the court will allow you to retain an asset brought into the marriage, but the following are questions the court will consider in making its determination if there is a dispute whether it is what the law calls "separate property":

- Can the premarital asset be clearly traced? For example, if you continue to own a vehicle that you brought into the marriage, it is likely that it will be awarded to you. However, if you brought a vehicle into the marriage, sold it during the marriage, and spent the proceeds, it is less likely that the court will consider awarding you its value.

- Did you keep the property separate and titled in your name, or did you commingle (mix) it with marital assets? Premarital assets you kept separate may be more likely to be awarded to you.

- Did the other spouse contribute to the increase in the value of the premarital asset, and can the value of that increase be proven? For example, suppose a woman owned a home prior to her marriage. After the marriage, the parties lived in the home, continuing to make mortgage payments and improvements to the home. At the time of the divorce, the husband seeks a portion of the equity in the home. The court might consider the value of the home at the time of the marriage, any contributions to the increase in equity made by the husband, and the evidence of the value of those contributions.

11.15 Will I get to keep my engagement ring?

Yes. When you went through with the marriage, the ring became yours.

11.16 Can I keep gifts and inheritances I received during the marriage?

Similar rules apply to gifts and inheritances received during the marriage as apply to premarital assets, that is, assets you owned prior to the marriage.

Gifts that you and your spouse gave to each other may be treated as any other marital asset. For gifts received during the marriage, such as a gift from a parent, the court will need to determine whether the gift was made to one party or to both. Whether you will be entitled to keep assets you inherited, assuming they are still in existence, will depend upon the unique circumstances of your case. When dividing the marital estate, the court may consider the fact that one spouse is allowed to keep substantial nonmarital assets such as an inheritance.

The following factors increase the probability that you will be entitled to keep your inheritance:

- It has been kept separate from the marital assets, such as in a separate account.
- It is titled in your name only.
- It can be clearly identified.
- It has not been commingled/mixed with marital assets.
- Your spouse has not contributed to its care, operation, or improvement.

It is less likely that you will be awarded your full inheritance if:

- It was commingled with marital assets.
- Its origin cannot be traced.
- You have placed your spouse's name on the title.
- Your spouse has contributed to the increase in the value of the inheritance.

Obviously this can be a complex issue. Talk to your attorney about their thoughts on your likelihood of success and what they will need as far as proof of ownership.

11.17 If my spouse and I can't decide who gets what, who decides? Can that person's decision be contested?

If you and your spouse cannot agree on the division of your property, the judge will make the determination, but you likely will have to go to mediation first.

If either party is dissatisfied with the decision reached by the judge, an appeal to a higher court is possible, but reversing the trial court in a divorce is a tough proposition.

11.18 What is a *property settlement agreement?*

A *property settlement agreement* is a written document that includes all of the financial agreements you and your spouse have reached in your divorce. This may include the division of property, debts, child support, alimony, insurance, and attorney fees.

The property settlement may be a separate document, or it may be incorporated into the decree of dissolution, which is the final court order dissolving your marriage.

11.19 How are the values of property determined?

The value of some assets, like bank accounts, are usually not disputed. The value of other assets, such as homes or personal property, are more likely to be disputed.

If your case proceeds to trial, you may give your opinion of the value of property you own. You or your spouse may also have certain property appraised by an expert. In such cases it may be necessary to have the appraiser appear at trial to give testimony regarding the appraisal and the value of the asset.

If you own substantial assets for which the value is likely to be disputed, talk to your attorney early in your case about the benefits and costs of expert witnesses.

11.20 What does *date of valuation* mean?

Because the value of assets can go up or down while a divorce is pending, it can be necessary to determine a set date for valuing the marital assets. This is referred to as the *date of valuation*. You and your spouse can agree on the date the assets should be valued. If you cannot agree, the judge will decide the date of valuation.

Among the most common dates used are the date of separation or the date of the filing of the divorce. The least likely used is the date of the divorce trial.

11.21 What happens after my spouse and I reach an agreement with the decree? Do we still have to go to court?

After you and your spouse sign your names to the decree, it must still be approved by your judge. Additionally, a judge should be reviewing the decree to make sure it is fair and equitable and if there are children that the decree provides for their best interest.

11.22 What happens to our individual checking and savings accounts during the divorce?

Regardless of whose name is on the account, bank accounts may be considered marital assets and may be divided by the court. Discuss with your attorney the benefits of a temporary restraining order to protect bank accounts, how to use these accounts while the case is pending, and the likely date of valuation.

11.23 Who gets the interest from certificates of deposit and dividends from stock holdings held during the divorce proceedings?

Whether you or your spouse receives interest from these assets is decided as a part of the overall division of your property and debts.

11.24 Do each one of our financial accounts have to be divided in half if we agree to an equal division of our assets?

No. Rather than incurring the administrative challenges and expense of dividing each asset in half, you and your spouse can decide that one of you will take certain assets equal to the value of assets taken by the spouse. If necessary, one of you can agree to make a cash payment to the other to make an equitable division.

11.25 What factors determine whether I can get at least half of my spouse's business?

Many factors determine whether you will get a share of your spouse's business and in what form you might receive it. Among the factors the court will look at are:

- Whether your spouse owned the business prior to your marriage
- Your role, if any, in operating the business or increasing its value
- If the business started during the marriage did the other spouse spend his or her time focusing on raising the children

If you or your husband own a business, it is important that you work with your attorney early in your case to develop a strategy for valuing the business and making your case for how it should be treated in the division of property and debts. It is common for couples to fight over the value of a business. Often, the non-operating spouse alleges it is worth a great deal, while the business operator argues the business has a lot of debt.

11.26 My husband and I have owned and run our own business together for many years. Can I be forced out of it?

Deciding what should happen with a family business when divorce occurs can be a challenge. Because of the risk for future conflict between you and your spouse, the value of the business is likely to be substantially decreased if you both remain owners.

In discussing your options with your lawyer, consider the following questions:

- If one spouse retains ownership of the business, are there enough other assets for the other spouse to receive a fair share of the total marital assets?
- Which spouse has the skills and experience to continue running the business?
- What would you do if you weren't working in the business?
- What is the value of the business?

- What is the market for the business if it were to be sold?
- Could you remain an employee of the business for some period of time even if you were not an owner?

You and your spouse know your business best. With the help of your lawyers, you may be able to create a settlement that can satisfy you both. If not, the judge will make the decision for you at trial.

11.27 I suspect my spouse is hiding assets, but I can't prove it. How can I protect myself if I discover later that I was right?

Make sure your lawyer has sent out subpoenas to third parties instead of relying only on your spouse's discovery responses. Consider whether you have the financial means to have a forensic accountant look for hidden assets.

Ask your lawyer to include language in your divorce decree to address your concern. Insist that it include an acknowledgment by your spouse that the agreement was based upon a full and complete disclosure of your spouse's financial condition. Discuss with your lawyer a provision that allows for setting aside the agreement if it is later discovered that assets were hidden.

11.28 My spouse says I'm not entitled to a share of his stock options because he gets to keep them only if he stays employed with his company. What are my rights?

Stock options are often a very valuable asset. They are also one of the most complex issues when dividing assets during a divorce for these and other reasons:

- Each company has its own rules about awarding and exercising stock options.
- Complete information is needed from the employer.
- There are different methods for calculating the value of stock options
- The reasons the options were given can impact the valuation. For example, some are given for future performance.

- There are cost and tax considerations when options are exercised.

Rather than being awarded a portion of the stock options themselves, you are likely to receive a share of the proceeds when the stock options are exercised.

Discuss this issue at the outset of the case with your counsel.

11.29 What is a *prenuptial agreement* and could it affect the property settlement phase of the divorce?

A *prenuptial agreement,* also referred to as an *antenuptial agreement,* is a contract entered into by the couple prior to their marriage. It can include provisions for how assets and debts will be divided in the event the marriage is terminated. It also lays out terms for alimony.

Your property settlement is likely to be impacted by the terms of your prenuptial agreement if the agreement is upheld as valid by the court.

11.30 Can a prenuptial agreement be contested during the divorce?

Yes, but understand this is a difficult task. The court may consider many factors in determining whether to uphold your prenuptial agreement. Among them are:

- Whether your agreement was entered into voluntarily
- Whether English is your spouse's first language
- Whether your agreement was fair and reasonable at the time it was signed
- Whether you and your spouse each gave a complete disclosure of your assets and debts
- Whether you and your spouse each had your own lawyer
- Whether you and your spouse each had enough time to consider the agreement

If you have a prenuptial agreement, take a copy of it to the initial consultation with your attorney. Be sure to provide your lawyer with a detailed history of the facts and circumstances surrounding reaching and signing the agreement.

11.31 How can I protect assets from being destroyed or hidden?

Consulting with an attorney before the filing of divorce can reduce the risk that assets will be hidden, transferred, or destroyed by your spouse. This is especially important if your spouse has a history of destroying property, incurring substantial debt, or transferring money without your knowledge.

Among the possible actions you and your attorney can consider together include:

- Placing your family heirlooms or other valuables in a safe location
- Transferring some portion of financial accounts prior to filing for divorce
- Preparing an inventory of the personal property
- Taking photographs or a video of the property
- Obtaining copies of important financial records or statements

Plans to leave the marital home should also be discussed in detail with your attorney, so that any actions taken early in your case are consistent with your ultimate goals. Ask your lawyer how a victim protective order being filed against you could impact these plans.

11.32 Who will get the frozen embryo that we have stored at the health clinic?

The law on this issue is not yet established in Oklahoma. The terms of your contract with the clinic may impact the rights you and your spouse have, so provide a copy of it to your attorney for review. If permissible under your contract, you and your spouse may want to consider donating the embryo to another couple.

11.33 Will debts be considered when determining the division of the property?

Yes. Courts look at a global picture in the division of assets and debts. The court will consider the marital debts when dividing the property. For example, if you are awarded a car valued at $12,000, but you owe a $10,000 debt on the same vehicle, the court will take that debt into consideration in the overall division of the assets. Similarly, if one spouse agrees to pay substantial marital credit card debt, this obligation may also be considered in the final determination of the division of property and debts.

If your spouse incurred debts that you believe should be his or her sole responsibility, tell your attorney. Some debts may be considered nonmarital and treated separately from other debts incurred during the marriage. For example, if your spouse spent large sums of money on gambling or illegal drugs without your knowledge, you may be able to argue that those debts should be the sole responsibility of your spouse.

11.34 What happens to the property distribution if one of us dies before the divorce proceedings are completed?

If your spouse dies prior to your divorce decree being entered, you will be considered married and treated as a surviving spouse under the law.

12

Benefits: Insurance, Retirement, and Pensions

During your marriage, you might have taken certain employment benefits for granted. You might not have given much thought each month to having insurance through your spouse's work. When you find yourself in a divorce, suddenly these benefits come to the forefront of your mind.

You might also, even unconsciously, have seen your own employment retirement benefits as belonging to you and not your spouse, referring to "my 401(k)" or "my pension." After all, you are the one who went to work every day to earn it, right?

When you divorce, some benefits arising from your spouse's employment will end, some may continue for a period of time, and others may be divided between you. Retirement funds, in particular, are often one of the most valuable marital assets to be divided in a divorce.

12.1 Will my children continue to have health coverage through my spouse's work even though we're divorcing?

Yes. There is specific language in the automatic temporary injunction that is served with the divorce petition that requires the spouse who has the insurance to keep everyone enrolled on that insurance. If you or the children are taken off the insurance, it is grounds for a contempt of court action.

12.2 Will I continue to have health insurance through my spouse's work after the divorce?

Probably not. You may have insurance for a relatively short period of time. Even if your spouse agrees to keep you insured, most companies will remove you as soon as they learn the divorce has been finalized.

You can look into COBRA insurance, but this coverage is often expensive. You may also want to consider using the benefits of the *Affordable Care Act (ACA)* at healthcare.gov. Because you will not have your spouse's income, you may qualify for subsidized health insurance through the ACA.

12.3 What is a *QMSO*?

A *qualified medical support order (QMSO)* is a court order providing continued group health insurance coverage for a minor child. A QMSO may also enable a parent to obtain other information about the plan without having to go through the parent who has the coverage. Rather than allowing only the parent with the insurance to be reimbursed for a claim, under a QMSO a health insurance plan is required to reimburse directly whoever actually paid the child's medical expense.

12.4 How many years must I have been married before I'm eligible to receive a part of my spouse's retirement fund or pension?

Even if your marriage is not of long duration, you may be entitled to a portion of your spouse's retirement fund or pension accumulated during the marriage. For example, if you were married for three years and your spouse contributed $10,000 to a 401(k) plan during the marriage, it is possible that the court would award you half of the value of the 401k when dividing your property and debts.

12.5 I contributed to my pension plan for ten years before I got married. Will my spouse get half of my entire pension?

No. It is considered separate property. If either you or your spouse made premarital contributions to a pension or retirement plan, be sure to let your attorney know. This information is essential in determining which portion of the retirement plan should be treated as "premarital"—assets that should not be shared.

12.6 I plan to keep my same job after my divorce. Will my former spouse get half of the money I contribute to my retirement plan after my divorce?

No. Your former spouse should be entitled to the portion of your retirement accumulated only during the marriage.

12.7 Am I still entitled to a share of my spouse's retirement even though I never contributed to one during our twenty-five-year marriage?

Probably. Retirements are often the most valuable asset accumulated during a marriage. Consequently, your judge will consider the retirement along with all of the other marital assets and debts when determining a fair division.

12.8 My lawyer says I'm entitled to a share of my spouse's retirement. How can I find out how much I get and when I'm eligible to receive it?

More than one factor will determine your rights to collect from your spouse's retirement. One factor will be the terms of the court order dividing the retirement. The court order will tell you whether you are entitled to a set dollar amount, a percentage, or a fraction to be determined based upon the length of your marriage and how long your spouse continues working.

Another factor will be the terms of the retirement plan itself. Some provide for lump sum withdrawals; others issue payments in monthly installments. Review the terms of your court order and contact the plan administrator to obtain the clearest understanding of your rights and benefits.

12.9 If I am eligible to receive my spouse's retirement benefits, must I be sixty-five years old to collect them?

It depends, but in many cases it is possible to begin receiving your share at the earliest date your spouse is eligible to receive them, regardless of whether he or she elects to do so. Check the terms of your spouse's plan to learn your options.

12.10 What happens if my former spouse is old enough to receive benefits but I'm not?

Ordinarily you will be eligible to begin receiving your share of the benefits when your former spouse begins his or hers. Depending upon the plan, you may be eligible to receive them sooner.

12.11 Am I entitled to *cost-of-living increases* on my share of my spouse's retirement?

It depends. If your spouse has a retirement plan that includes a provision for a *cost-of-living allowance (COLA)*, talk to your lawyer about whether this can be included in the court order dividing the retirement.

12.12 What circumstances might prevent my getting part of my spouse's retirement benefits?

Some government pension plans are not subject to division. If you or your spouse are employed by a government agency, talk with your lawyer about how this may affect the property settlement in your case.

12.13 Does the death of my spouse affect the payout of retirement benefits to me or to our children?

It depends upon both the nature of your spouse's retirement plan and the terms of the court order dividing the retirement. If you want to be eligible for survivorship benefits from your spouse's pension, discuss the issue with your attorney before your case is settled or goes to trial. He or she can advise you.

Some plans allow only a surviving spouse or former spouse to be a beneficiary. Others may allow for the naming of an alternate beneficiary, such as your children.

12.14 How do I receive my half of my spouse's retirement?

Retirement accounts must be divided between the two spouses by a legal instrument known as a *qualified domestic relations order (QDRO)*. In the case of a federal retirement plan, it's called a *court order acceptable for processing (COAP)*. The purpose of these legal instruments is to allow a spouse's retirement account to be divided so that some portion of that retirement goes to the other spouse. At the time the funds are received, if the receiving spouse invests the funds back into a retirement account, such as an IRA, no taxes will be due. However, if the receiving spouse spends the money, he or she will be taxed and the amount of taxation could quite high.

If you are the party receiving the retirement funds your lawyer will be responsible for drafting the QDRO or COAP. Having these instruments drafted is often expensive because they are complex and there is no standardized form. Often, the first draft of the QDRO is rejected by the retirement plan administrator and revisions are required. Be diligent in following up with your lawyer to ensure the document is drafted.

Nowadays, more companies are devising their own forms that allow the parties to divide retirement accounts without the expense and complexity of a QDRO.

12.15 If my former spouse passes on before I do, can I still collect his or her Social Security benefits?

It depends. If you were married to your spouse for ten or more years and you have not remarried, you may be eligible for benefits. Contact your local Social Security Administration office or visit the SSA website at www.ssa.gov.

12.16 What orders might the court enter regarding life insurance?

The judge may order you or your spouse to maintain a life insurance policy to ensure that future support payments are made if alimony is ordered. In most cases you will be required to pay for your own life insurance after your divorce, and you should include this as an expense in your monthly budget.

12.17 Because we share children, should I consider my spouse as a beneficiary on my life insurance?

It depends upon your intentions. If your intention is to give the money to your former spouse, by all means name the other parent as beneficiary.

However, if you intend the life insurance proceeds to be used for the benefit of your children, talk with your attorney about your options. You may consider naming a trustee to manage the life insurance proceeds on behalf of your children, and there may be reasons to choose someone other than your former spouse.

12.18 My spouse is in the military. What are my rights to benefits after the divorce?

As the former spouse of a military member, the types of benefits to which you may be entitled are typically determined by the number of years you were married, the number of years your spouse was in the military while you were married, and whether you have remarried. Be sure you obtain accurate information about these dates.

Among the benefits you may be eligible are:

- A portion of your spouse's military retirement pay
- A survivor benefit in the event of your spouse's death
- Health care or participation in a temporary, transitional health care program
- Use of certain military facilities, such as the commissary

While your divorce is pending, educate yourself about your right to future military benefits so that you can plan for your future with clarity. Contact your base legal office or, for more information, visit the website for the branch of the military of which your spouse was a member.

13

Division of Debts

Throughout a marriage, most couples will have disagreements about money from time to time. You might think extra money should be spent on a family vacation, and your spouse might insist it should be saved for your retirement. You might think it's time you finally get a new car, and your spouse thinks you would be fine driving the ten-year-old van for two more years.

If you and your spouse had different philosophies about saving and spending during your marriage, chances are you will have some differing opinions when dividing your debts in divorce. Regardless of how the debts from your marriage are divided, know that you will gradually build your independent financial success when making a fresh start after your divorce is final.

13.1   Who is responsible for paying credit card bills and making house payments during the divorce proceedings?

In most cases the court will not make decisions regarding the payment of credit card debt on a temporary basis. Work with your attorney and your spouse to reach a temporary agreement. Discuss the importance of making at least minimum payments on time to avoid substantial finance charges and late fees.

Typically, the spouse who remains in the home will be responsible for the mortgage payments, taxes, utilities, and most other ordinary expenses related to the house.

If you are concerned that you cannot afford to stay in the marital home on a temporary basis, talk with your attorney about your options prior to your temporary order hearing.

13.2 What, if anything, should I be doing with the credit card companies as we go through the divorce?

Begin by obtaining a copy of your credit report from at least two of the three nationwide consumer reporting companies: Experian, Equifax, and TransUnion. The Fair Credit Reporting Act entitles you to a free copy of your credit report from each of these three companies every twelve months.

To order your free annual report online, go to www.annualcreditreport.com, call toll free to (877) 322-8228, or complete an Annual Credit Report Request Form and mail it to: Annual Credit Report Request Service, P.O. Box 105283, Atlanta, Georgia 30348-5283. You can print the form from the Federal Trade Commission website at www.ftc.gov/credit. You can receive a scored credit bureau report for free from www.creditkarma.com. This is an excellent tool to see how banks rate you.

Your spouse may have incurred debt using your name and signed an application you are unaware of. This information is important to relay to your attorney. If you and your spouse have joint credit card accounts, contact any credit card company to close the account. Do the same if your spouse is an authorized user on any of your accounts.

If you want to maintain credit with a company, ask to have a new account in your own name. Be sure to let your spouse know if you close an account he or she has been using.

13.3 How is credit card debt divided?

Credit card debt will be divided as a part of the overall division of the marital property and debts. Just as in the division of property, the court considers what is equitable, or fair, in your case.

If your spouse has exclusively used a credit card for purposes that did not benefit the family, such as gambling, talk with your attorney. In most cases the court will not review a lengthy history of how you and your spouse used the credit cards, but there can be exceptions.

13.4   Am I responsible for repayment of my spouse's student loans?

It depends. If your spouse incurred student loans prior to the marriage, it is most likely that he or she will be ordered to pay that debt.

If the debt was incurred during the marriage, how the funds were used may have an impact on who is ordered to pay them. For example, if your spouse borrowed $3,000 during the marriage for tuition, it is likely your spouse will be ordered to pay that debt. However, if a $3,000 student loan was taken out by your spouse, but $1,000 of it was used for a family vacation, then the court would be more likely to order the debt shared.

If either you or your spouse has student loan debt, be sure to give your attorney the complete history regarding the debt and ask about the most likely outcome under the facts of your case.

13.5   During the divorce proceedings, am I still responsible for debt my spouse continues to accrue?

In most cases the court will order each of the parties to be responsible for his or her own post-separation debts.

13.6   During the marriage my spouse applied for and received several credit cards without my knowledge. Am I responsible for them?

It depends. The court will consider the overall fairness of the property and debt division when deciding who should pay this debt. If your spouse bought items with the cards and plans to keep those items, it is likely that she or he will be ordered to pay the debt incurred for the purchases.

13.7   During our marriage, we paid off thousands of dollars of debt incurred by my spouse before we were married. Will the court take this into consideration when dividing our property and debt?

It might. Just as premarital assets can have an impact on the overall division of property and debts, so can premarital debt. Depending upon the length of the marriage, the evidence of the debt, and the amount paid, it may be a factor for the judge to consider.

Be sure to let your attorney know if either you or your spouse brought substantial debt into the marriage and what happened to it.

13.8 Regarding debts, what is a *hold-harmless clause,* and why should it be in the divorce decree? What are the clause's limitations if a debt is not refinanced?

A *hold-harmless provision* is intended to protect you in the event that your spouse fails to follow a court order to pay a debt after the divorce is granted. The language typically provides that your spouse shall "indemnify and hold (you) harmless from liability" on the debt. Typically, the house will be awarded to one of the parties with the provision that the spouse receiving the house will remove the other spouse's name from the mortgage and note and obtain a new mortgage and note solely in her or his name.

Understand that if the mortgage is not refinanced in your ex-spouse's name, a lender can still come after you for the mortgage debt if your former spouse does not pay. Your only recourse at this point would be to file for contempt. However, if your ex-spouse files for bankruptcy, it is unlikely the court would find that your former spouse has the ability to pay, and your ex-spouse would be found not guilty of the contempt.

13.9 My spouse and I have agreed that I will keep our home; why must I refinance the mortgage?

There may be a number of reasons why your spouse is asking you to refinance the mortgage. First, the mortgage company cannot be forced to take your spouse's name off of the mortgage note. This means that if you did not make the house payments, the lender could pursue collection against your spouse.

Second, your spouse may not want to wait to receive a share of the home equity. It may be possible for you to borrow additional money at the time of refinancing to pay your spouse his or her share of the equity in the home.

Third, the mortgage on your family home may prevent your spouse from buying a home in the future. Because there remains a risk that your spouse could be pursued for the debt to the mortgage company, it is unlikely that a second lender will want to take the risk of extending further credit to your spouse.

13.10   Can I file for bankruptcy while my divorce is pending?

Consult with your attorney if you are considering filing for bankruptcy while your divorce is pending. It will be important for you to ask yourself a number of questions, such as:

- Should I file for bankruptcy on my own or with my spouse?
- How will my filing for bankruptcy affect my ability to purchase a home in the future?
- Which debts can be discharged in bankruptcy, and which cannot?
- How will a bankruptcy affect the division of property and debts in the divorce?
- How might a delay in the divorce proceedings due to a bankruptcy impact my case?
- Which form of bankruptcy is best for my situation?

If you use a different attorney for your bankruptcy than you have for your divorce, be sure that each attorney is kept fully informed about the developments in the other case.

13.11   What happens if my spouse files for bankruptcy during our divorce?

Contact your attorney right away. The filing of a bankruptcy while your divorce is pending can have a significant impact on your divorce. Your attorney can advise you whether certain debts are likely to be discharged in the bankruptcy, the delay a bankruptcy may cause to your divorce, and whether bankruptcy is an appropriate option for you.

13.12   Can I file for divorce while I am in bankruptcy?

Yes. However, you must receive the bankruptcy court's approval with the divorce. While in bankruptcy, your property is protected from debt collection by the automatic stay. The stay can also prevent the divorce court from dividing property between you and your spouse until you obtain the bankruptcy court's permission to proceed with the divorce.

13.13 What should I do if my former spouse files for bankruptcy after our divorce?

Contact your attorney immediately. If you learn that your former spouse has filed for bankruptcy, you may have certain rights to object to the discharge of any debts your spouse was ordered to pay under your divorce decree. If you fail to take action, it is possible that you will be held responsible for debts your spouse was ordered to pay.

14

Taxes

When your divorce is over, you want to be sure that you don't later discover you owe taxes you weren't expecting to pay. A number of tax issues may arise in your divorce. Most divorce and family law attorneys have limited tax knowledge, so consult with a certified public accountant regarding any complex tax questions during your divorce.

Taxes are important considerations in both settlement negotiations and trial preparation. They should not be overlooked. Taxes can impact many of your decisions, including those regarding alimony, division of property, and the receipt of benefits.

Be sure to ask the professionals helping you about the tax implications in your divorce so you don't get that letter in the mail that begins, "Dear Taxpayer:...."

14.1　Will either my spouse or I have to pay income tax when we transfer property or pay a property settlement to each other according to our divorce decree?

No. However, it is important that you see the future tax consequences of a subsequent withdrawal, sale, or transfer of certain assets you receive in your divorce. It is important to ask your attorney to take tax consequences into consideration when looking at the division of your assets.

14.2　Is the amount of child support I pay tax deductible?

No.

14.3 Do I have to pay income tax on any child support I receive?

No. Your child support is tax-free regardless of when it is paid or when it is received.

14.4 Is the amount of alimony I am ordered to pay tax deductible?

Yes. Spousal support paid according to a court order is deductible. This includes court-ordered alimony and may also include other forms of support provided to your former spouse (but not child support). Your tax deduction is a factor to consider when determining a fair amount of alimony to be paid in your case.

14.5 Must I pay tax on the alimony I receive?

Yes. You must pay income tax on the spousal support you receive. This will include court-ordered alimony and may also include other forms of spousal support, but not child support, paid by your spouse.

As mentioned, income tax is a critical factor in determining a fair amount of alimony. Insist that your attorney bring this issue to the attention of your spouse's lawyer or to the judge, if your case proceeds to trial, so that both the tax you pay and the deduction your spouse receives are taken into consideration.

Be sure to consult with your tax advisor about payment of tax on your spousal support. Budgeting for and making the estimated tax payments throughout the year or withholding additional taxes from your wages can avoid a burdensome tax liability at the end of the year.

14.6 During the divorce proceedings, is our tax filing status affected?

It can be. You are considered unmarried if your decree is final by December 31 of the tax year.

If you are considered unmarried, your filing status is either "single" or, under certain circumstances, "head of household." If your decree is not final as of December 31, your filing status is either "married filing a joint return" or "married filing a separate return," unless you live apart from your spouse and meet the exception for "head of household."

While your divorce is in progress, talk to both your tax advisor and your attorney about your filing status. It may be beneficial to figure your tax on both a joint return and a separate return to see which gives you the lower tax. IRS Publication 504, Divorced or Separated Individuals (available at the IRS website, www.irs.gov), provides more detail on tax issues while you are going through a divorce.

14.7 Should I file a joint income tax return with my spouse while our divorce is pending?

Consult your tax advisor to determine the risks and benefits of filing of a joint return with your spouse. Compare this with the consequences of filing your tax return separately. Often the overall tax liability will be less with the filing of a joint return, but other factors are important to consider.

When deciding whether to file a joint return with your spouse, consider any concerns you have about the accuracy of the information your spouse may be providing. If you have any doubts, consult both your attorney and your tax advisor before agreeing to sign a joint tax return with your spouse. Prior to filing a return with your spouse, try to reach agreement about how any tax owed or refund will be divided. This can also work as an equalization tool in property settlement if one spouse keeps the entire return.

14.8 For tax purposes, is one time of year better to divorce than another?

It depends upon your tax situation. If you and your spouse agree that it would be beneficial to file joint tax returns for the year in which you are divorcing, you may wish to not have your divorce finalized before the end of the year.

Your marital status for filing income taxes is determined by your status on December 31. Consequently, if you both want to preserve your right to file a joint return, your decree should not be entered before December 1 of that year.

14.9 What tax consequences should I consider regarding the sale of our home?

When your home is sold, whether during your divorce or after, the sale may be subject to a capital gains tax. If your home was your primary residence and you lived in the home for two of the preceding five years, you may be eligible to exclude up to $250,000 of the gain on the sale of your home. If both you and your spouse meet the ownership and residence tests, you may be eligible to exclude up to $500,000 of the gain.

If you anticipate the gain on the sale of your residence to be over $250,000, talk with your attorney early in the divorce process about a plan to minimize the tax liability. For more information, see IRS Publication 523, Selling Your Home (available at the IRS website, www.irs.gov) and talk with your tax advisor.

14.10 How might capital gains tax be a problem for me years after the divorce?

Future capital gains tax on the sale of property should be discussed with your attorney during the negotiation and trial preparation stages of your case. This is especially important if the sale of the property is imminent. Failure to do so may result in an unfair outcome.

For example, suppose you agree that your spouse will be awarded the proceeds from the sale of your home valued at $200,000 after the real estate commission, and you will take the stock portfolio also valued at $200,000.

Suppose that after the divorce, you decide to sell the stock. It is still valued at $200,000, but you learn that its original price was $120,000 and that you must pay capital gains tax of 15 percent on the $80,000 of gain. You pay tax of $12,000, leaving you with $188,000.

Meanwhile, your former spouse sells the marital home but pays no capital gains tax because he qualifies for the $250,000 exemption. He is left with the full $200,000.

Tax implications of your property division should always be discussed with your attorney, with support from your tax advisor as needed.

14.11 During and after the divorce, who gets to claim the children as dependents?

The trend has now moved to alternate the federal income dependency exemption regardless of who has custody. Typically, the deduction will go according to odd-even years, so Dad may get the deduction in even years and Mom gets it in odd years. Generally, the party who pays the child support will be required to be current by December 31 on child support in order to get the deduction for their taxable year.

Another common practice if there is more than one child is to allow both spouses to claim one of the children each year. For example, if there are three children, one year Dad claims two and Mom claims one and the next year Mom will claim two and Dad will claim one.

14.12 My decree says I have to sign IRS Form 8332 so my former spouse can claim our child as an exemption because I have custody. Should I sign it once for all future years?

No. Child custody and child support can be modified in the future. If there is a future modification of custody or support, which parent is entitled to claim your child as an exemption could change. The best practice is to provide your former spouse with a timely copy of Form 8332 signed by you for the appropriate tax year only.

14.13 Can my spouse and I split the child-care tax credit?

The value of the federal child-care tax credit must be subtracted from the actual costs of child care to arrive at a figure for net child-care expenses owed by the spouse paying support.

Only the custodial parent is allowed to claim the credit. If you are a noncustodial parent and paying child care, talk to your lawyer about how to address this issue in your divorce decree.

14.14 Is the cost of getting a divorce, including my attorney fees, tax deductible under any circumstances?

Your legal fees for getting a divorce are not deductible. However, a portion of your attorney fees may be deductible if they are for:

- The collection of sums included in your gross income, such as alimony or interest income
- Advice regarding the determination of taxes or tax due

Attorney fees are "miscellaneous" deductions for individuals and are consequently are limited to 2 percent of your adjusted gross income. More details can be found in IRS Publication 529, Miscellaneous Deductions (available at the IRS website, www.irs.gov).

You may also be able to deduct fees you pay to appraisers or accountants who help. Talk to your tax advisor about whether any portion of your attorney fees or other expenses from your divorce are deductible.

14.15 Do I have to complete a new Form W-4 for my employer because of my divorce?

Completing a new Form W-4, Employee's Withholding Certificate, will help you to claim the proper withholding allowances based upon your marital status and exemptions. Also, if you are receiving alimony, you may need to make quarterly estimated tax payments. Consult with your tax advisor to ensure you are making the most preferable tax planning decision.

14.16 What is innocent spouse relief and how can it help me?

If you filed a joint return with your spouse, but subsequently learned the information was fraudulent or inaccurate, innocent spouse relief is a program designed to prevent you from being penalized for the information that you were unaware of. Numerous factors affect your eligibility for innocent spouse tax relief, such as:

- You would suffer a financial hardship if you were required to pay the tax.
- You did not significantly benefit from the unpaid taxes.
- You suffered abuse during your marriage.
- You thought your spouse would pay the taxes on the original return.

You may benefit from a referral to an attorney who specializes in tax law. At a minimum, speak to a certified public accountant.

15

Going to Court

For many people, the idea of going to court can be frightening. This is a normal reaction. Recognize, though, that court is fairly different from what we see on TV and the movies. There is often a lot more waiting and a lot less drama.

Understanding what will occur in court and being well prepared for any court hearings will relieve much of your stress. Knowing the order of events, courtroom etiquette, the role of the people in the courtroom, and what is expected of you will make the entire experience easier.

Your lawyer will be with you at all times to support you any time you go to court. Remember, every court appearance moves you one step closer to completing your divorce so that you can move forward with your life.

15.1 What do I need to know about appearing in court and court dates in general?

Court dates are important. As soon as you receive a notice from your attorney about a court date in your case, confirm whether your attendance will be required and put it on your calendar.

Ask your attorney about the nature of the hearing, including whether the judge will be listening to testimony by witnesses, or whether the lawyers will simply argue in chambers (the judge's office). Inquire whether you are expected to bring any documents like copies of your paychecks.

Ask whether it is necessary for you to meet with your attorney before court or to take any other action to prepare for the hearing, such as providing additional information or documents.

Find out how long the hearing is expected to last. It may be as short as a few minutes or as long as a day or more. If you want someone to go to court with you to provide you support, check with your attorney first.

15.2   When and how often will I need to go to court?

Whether and how often you will need to go to court depends upon a number of factors. Depending upon the complexity of your case, you may have only one hearing or numerous court hearings throughout the course of your divorce.

Some hearings, usually those on procedural matters, are attended only by the attorneys. These could include requests for the other side to provide information or for the setting of certain deadlines. These hearings are often brief and held in the judge's chambers rather than in the courtroom. Other hearings, such as temporary hearings for custody or support, are typically attended by both parties and their attorneys.

If you and your spouse settle or reach an agreement on all of the issues in your case, a hearing on the decree will be held and generally one spouse along with their lawyer will attend.

15.3   How much notice will I get about appearing in court?

Unless it is an emergency hearing, you should always have at least ten days' notice for a final divorce trial. Typically, they are set many weeks, if not months, in advance. If you receive a notice of a hearing, contact your attorney immediately. He or she can tell you whether your appearance is required and what other steps are needed to prepare.

15.4   I am afraid to be alone in the same room with my spouse. When I go to court, is this going to happen if the lawyers go into the judge's office to discuss the case?

Prior to any court hearing, you and your spouse may be asked to wait while your attorneys meet with the judge to discuss preliminary matters.

A number of options are likely to be available to ensure that you feel safe. These might include having you and your spouse wait in different locations or having a friend or family member present. Tell your lawyer your concerns so that he or she can help you feel safe throughout court proceedings.

15.5   Do I have to go to court every time there is a court hearing on any motion?

Not necessarily. Some matters will be decided by the judge after listening to the arguments of the lawyers. These hearings are usually held in the judge's chambers, and you will not be required to attend.

15.6   My spouse's lawyer keeps asking for *continuances of court dates.* Is there anything I can do to stop this?

Continuances of court dates are not unusual in divorces. A court date might be postponed many reasons, including a conflict on the calendar of one of the attorneys or the judge, the lack of availability of one of the parties or an important witness, or the need for more time to prepare.

Discuss with your attorney your desire to move your case forward without further delay so that repeated requests for continuances can be vigorously resisted.

15.7   If I have to go to court, will I be put on the stand? Will there be a jury?

You will be put on the witness stand. Even if your lawyer does not call you, your spouse's attorney will. There will not be a jury; your case will be heard by a judge.

15.8   My lawyer said I need to be in court for our temporary hearing next week. What's going to happen?

A temporary hearing is held to determine such matters as who remains in the house while your divorce is pending, temporary custody, and temporary child support.

In some counties, your hearing will be one of several other hearings. You may find yourself in a courtroom with many other lawyers and their clients, all having matters scheduled before the court that day. Some judges place severe limitations on the amount of time for a temporary hearing, such as one hour per party.

If temporary custody is disputed, you and other witnesses will take the witness stand to give testimony at your temporary hearing. If this is the case, meeting with your attorney in advance to fully prepare is very important.

15.9 Are there any rules about courtroom etiquette that I need to know?

Knowing the following tips about being in the courtroom will make your experience easier.

- Dress appropriately. Avoid overly casual dress, lots of jewelry, revealing clothing, and extreme hairstyles.
- Don't bring beverages into the courtroom. Most courts do not allow food and drink in courtrooms. If you need water, tell your lawyer.
- Dispose of chewing gum before giving testimony.
- Don't talk aloud in the courtroom unless you're on the witness stand or being questioned by the judge.
- Stand up whenever the judge is entering or leaving the courtroom.
- Be sure to turn off your cell phone.

Although you may feel anxious initially, you'll likely feel more relaxed about the courtroom setting once your hearing gets underway.

15.10 Will there be a court reporter, and what will he or she do?

The court reporter officially records the testimony that occurs in court and he or she also receives evidence admitted in court. Unless both parties waive having a court reporter, which is rare, a court reporter will be present. If a dispute occurs over what was said or one of the sides wants to file an appeal, the record that the court reporter makes will be sent to the appellate court.

15.11 Will I be able to talk to my attorney while we are in court?

During court proceedings it is important that your attorney give his or her full attention to anything being said by the judge, witnesses, or your spouse's lawyer. For this reason, your attorney will avoid talking with you when anyone else in the courtroom is speaking. It is important that your attorney focus on the testimony.

Plan to have a pen and paper at hand so that you can write notes or questions to your attorney.

If your court hearing is lengthy, breaks will be taken. You can use this time to discuss with your attorney any questions or observations you have about the proceeding.

15.12 What questions might the judge ask me at the final hearing about the problems in our marriage and why I want the divorce?

This is almost never an issue. Oklahoma, like most states, is a no-fault state and the judge doesn't care why you are divorcing unless it relates to the best interest of the children. Even if your spouse doesn't want the divorce, if you indicate that you want the divorce the judge will grant you the divorce.

15.13 My lawyer said that the judge wants a *pretrial order* having to do with my upcoming trial and that we'll have to "comply" with it. What does this mean?

A *pretrial order* is designed to make the trial easier for the judge. The two lawyers get together and create the pretrial order. This might include:

- A list of issues that have been settled
- A list of issues that are still disputed
- Agreements, referred to as *stipulations,* as to the truth of certain facts
- The names of witnesses
- Exhibits
- A summary of how you want the judge to decide the case

Deadlines are given for providing the information.

15.14 What is a *pretrial conference?*

A *pretrial conference* is a meeting held with the lawyers and the judge to review information related to an upcoming trial. They will discuss such things as how long the trial is expected to last, the issues in dispute, and the law surrounding the disputed issues. Often this is done in the judge's chambers.

The most significant thing that occurs is the setting of the actual divorce trial date. Not all judges require you to attend the pretrial conference. Ask your attorney whether you need to attend.

15.15 Besides meeting with my lawyer, is there anything else I should do to prepare for my upcoming trial?

Yes. Be sure to review any depositions (if taken) and any information you provided in your discovery, such as answers to interrogatories, as well as your proposed division of assets and liabilities. At trial, it is possible that you will be asked some of the same questions that you were asked in your deposition. If you think you might give different answers at trial, discuss this with your lawyer.

It is important that your attorney know in advance of trial whether any information you provided during the discovery process has changed.

15.16 I'm meeting with my lawyer to prepare for trial. How do I make the most of these meetings?

Write out your questions regarding topics such as custody, child support, division of assets, and what exhibits you will be expected to talk about. Confirm which of your witnesses need subpoenas and which ones do not. Ask what areas your lawyer has concerns about. Ask your attorney if he or she is concerned about topics the other attorney may bring up. Inquire what you need to know about the judge.

15.17 My lawyer says that the law firm is busy with "trial preparation." What exactly is my lawyer doing to prepare for my trial?

Countless tasks are necessary to perform to prepare your case for trial. Following are just some of them:

- Developing arguments to be made on each of the contested issues
- Researching and reviewing the relevant law in your case
- Reviewing the facts of your case to determine which witnesses are best suited to testifying about them
- Reviewing, selecting, preparing, and copying exhibits
- Preparing questions for all witnesses
- Reviewing discovery responses from both sides
- Determining the order of witnesses and all exhibits
- Preparing your file for the day of court

Your lawyer is committed to a good outcome for you in your divorce. He or she will be engaged in many important actions to fully prepare your case for trial.

15.18 My divorce is scheduled for trial. Does this mean there is no hope for a settlement?

Many cases are settled after a trial date is set. The setting of a trial date may cause you and your spouse to think about the risks and costs of going to trial. This can help both of you focus on what is most important to you and lead you toward a negotiated settlement. Because the costs of preparing for and proceeding to trial are substantial, it is best to engage in settlement negotiations well in advance of your trial date.

15.19 Can I prevent my spouse from being in the courtroom?

No. He or she has a legal right to be there.

15.20 Can I take a friend or family member with me to court?

It depends upon whether they will be witnesses in your case. In some cases, where witnesses other than the husband and wife are testifying, the attorneys request that the court "sequester" the witnesses. The judge could then order all witnesses, except you and your spouse, to leave the courtroom until after they have testified. Once a witness has completed his or her testimony, he or she will ordinarily be allowed to remain in the courtroom for the remainder of the trial.

Let your attorney know in advance if you intend to bring anyone to court with you.

15.21 I want to do a great job testifying as a witness in my divorce trial. What are some tips?

Keep the following in mind to be a good witness on your own behalf:

- Tell the truth. While this may not always be comfortable, it is critical if you want your testimony to be believed by the judge.

- Listen carefully to the complete question before thinking of your answer. Wait to consider your answer until after the full question is asked.

- Think about whether you are actually answering the question being asked or are you are trying to turn your answer into a response about your spouse. This is a common problem that irritates judges. Don't do it.

- If you don't understand a question or don't know the answer, be sure to say so.

- If the question calls for a "yes" or "no" answer, simply say so. Then wait for the attorney to ask you the next question. If there is more you want to explain, remember that you have already told your attorney all of the important facts and he or she will make sure you are allowed to give any testimony significant in your case.

- Don't argue with the judge or the lawyers.

- Try to keep the same pace throughout; a slow pace is best. If you state very quickly what your salary is but on tougher questions you take long pauses, you might create the impression that you are making something up. You can avoid this problem by keep a slow pace throughout.

- Stop speaking if an objection is made by one of the lawyers. Wait until the judge has decided whether to allow you to answer.

15.22 Should I be worried about being cross-examined by my spouse's lawyer at trial?

Focus not on worry but on preparation. Your lawyer can probably tell you what potential topics you need to focus on. You might do some role-playing with your lawyer and another lawyer in the office playing the role of your spouse's attorney. Tell your lawyer in the mock session to be extra tough on you. This will make the actual experience much easier. Try not to take the questions personally; your lawyer is only trying to help you prepare.

15.23 What happens on the day of trial?

Although no two trials are alike, the following steps will occur in most divorce trials.

- Attorneys meet with judge in chambers to discuss procedural issues, such as how many witnesses will be called, how long the case will take to present, and when breaks might be taken.
- Attorneys may give opening statements. However, many judges prefer not to hear them.
- Petitioner's attorney calls petitioner's witnesses to testify. Respondent's attorney may cross-examine each of them.
- Respondent's attorney calls respondent's witnesses to testify. Petitioner's attorney may cross-examine each of them.
- Petitioner's lawyer calls any rebuttal witnesses, that is, witnesses whose testimony contradicts the testimony of the respondent's witnesses.
- Closing arguments are made.

15.24 Will the judge decide my case the day I go to court?

Some judges provide a decision at that time. A judge may take a short break at the conclusion of the hearing to make his or her decision. If your matter is complex and contentious, it is very likely the matter will be taken under advisement (the status of a case when the judge has not yet made a decision) and a ruling will be made in a couple of weeks. Typically, the decision is issued in writing and you are not required to return to court.

16

The Appeals Process

You may find that, despite your best efforts to settle your case, your divorce went to trial and the judge made major decisions that will have a serious impact on your future. You may be gravely disappointed or even shocked by the judge's ruling.

The judge might have seen your case differently than you and your attorney did. Perhaps the judge made mistakes.

Whatever the reasons for the court's rulings, you may feel that the judge's decisions are not ones that you can live with. If this is the case, talk to your lawyer immediately about your right to appeal. Together you can decide whether an appeal is in your best interest, or whether it is better to accept the court's ruling and invest your energy in moving forward with your future without an appeal.

16.1 How much time after my divorce do I have to file an appeal?

You must commence the appeal within thirty days of the date that the decree is filed. Because your attorney may also recommend filing certain motions following your trial, discuss your appeal rights with your lawyer as soon as you have received the judge's ruling. Do not wait until day twenty-eight to tell your lawyer you have decided to appeal. You must let him or her know as soon as possible.

16.2 Can I appeal a temporary order?

No.

16.3   What parts of the decree can be appealed?

Almost any aspect of the decision can be appealed; however, the likelihood of success will probably be limited to one or two issues.

16.4   If I appeal, what facts will the appellate court look at to possibly reverse the trial judge's decision?

The appellate court would look at a standard known as an abuse of discretion standard. However, a judge can make a wrong decision or even a decision different from what the appellate court would have made without it being considered an abuse of discretion. There is a presumption the trial court ruled correctly, and you need to show with objective evidence why it was wrong.

16.5   Will my attorney recommend that I appeal specific aspects of the decree, or will I have to request it?

Your attorney may counsel you to file an appeal on certain issues of your case. But if your attorney tells you that you have a very low probability of success with an appeal, you should weigh heavily what they say.

16.6   When should an appeal be filed?

An appeal should be filed only after careful consultation with your lawyer when you and your attorney believe that the judge has made a serious error under the law or the facts of your case. Among the factors you and your attorney should discuss are:

- Whether the judge had authority under the law to make the decisions set forth in your decree
- The likelihood of the success of your appeal
- The risk that an appeal by you will encourage an appeal by your former spouse
- The cost of an appeal
- The length of time an appeal can be expected to take
- The impact of a delay in the case during the appeal

As stated earlier, the deadline for filing an appeal is thirty days from the date that a final order is filed in your case.

16.7 Are there any disadvantages to filing an appeal?

There can be disadvantages to filing an appeal, including:

- Increased attorney fees and costs
- Prolonged conflict between you and your former spouse
- The delay itself
- The risk of a worse outcome on appeal than you received at trial
- Difficulty in obtaining closure and moving forward with your life
- Most divorce appeals are denied

16.8 Is an attorney necessary to appeal?

The appeals process is very detailed and specific, with set deadlines and specific court rules. Given the complex nature of the appellate process, you should have an attorney if you intend to file an appeal.

16.9 How long does the appeals process usually take?

It will take an average of sixteen to twenty-two months.

16.10 What are the steps in the appeals process?

There are many steps your lawyer will take on your behalf in the appeals process, including:

- Identifying the issues to be appealed
- Filing a notice with the court of your intent to appeal
- Obtaining the necessary court documents and trial exhibits to send to the appellate court
- Obtaining a transcript of the trial, a written copy of testimony by witnesses and statements by the judge and the lawyers made in the presence of the court reporter
- Performing legal research to support your arguments on appeal
- Preparing and filing a document known as a *brief,* which sets forth the facts of the case and the relevant law, complete with citations to court transcripts, court documents, and prior cases

16.11   Is filing and pursuing an appeal expensive?

Yes. In addition to lawyer fees, there are filing fees as well as court reporter fees for transcripts.

16.12   If I do not file an appeal, can I ever go back to court to change my decree?

Certain aspects of a decree are not modifiable, such as the division of property and debts or the award of attorney fees. Other parts of your decree, such as child support or matters regarding the children, may be modified if there has been a "permanent, substantial and material change in conditions."

A modification of custody or visitation for minor children will also require you to show that the change would be in their best interest. Alimony is modifiable under certain conditions, such as remarriage or substantial changes in income.

Appendix

Sample Petition for Divorce

IN THE DISTRICT COURT OF _____ COUNTY
STATE OF OKLAHOMA

IN THE MARRIAGE OF	)	
	)	
JOHN DOE, PETITIONER	)	
	)	FD-2016-74
vs.	)	
	)	
JANE DOE, RESPONDENT	)	
	)	

COMES NOW the Petitioner, John Doe, by and through his attorney of record, Mark Antinoro, and for his cause of action against the Respondent, alleges and states as follows:

1. That the Petitioner has resided in Oklahoma for more than six consecutive months immediately preceding the filing hereof and this Court has dissolution of marriage/divorce subject matter jurisdiction and venue is proper herein.
2. That the address of the Petitioner is 604 XYZ Street, Pryor, Mayes County, Oklahoma 74361.
3. That the address of the Respondent is 318 South Blank Avenue, Pryor, Mayes County, Oklahoma 74361.
4. That neither party is a member of the armed forces for the United States or its allies.

Sample Petition for Divorce (Continued)

5. That neither the Petitioner nor the Respondent is a party to any other pending action for annulment, separation, or dissolution of marriage.
6. That the parties hereto were married in Broken Bow, Oklahoma on or about the 15th day of June, 1990.
7. That there are two minor children born of the marriage of the parties whose custody and welfare may be affected by these proceedings, to wit: Janet Lynn Doe, born May 19, 1994, age 11; and Robert Paul Doe, born December 12, 1996, age 8.
8. That the address of the minor children of the parties over the last five years was 318 South Blank Avenue, Pryor, Oklahoma 74361.
9. Oklahoma is the "home state" of the parties' minor children and each of them as that phrase is defined by Oklahoma's Uniform Child Custody Jurisdiction and Enforcement Act, 43 O.S. §551-101 et seq., and by the federal Parental Kidnapping Prevention Act, 28 U.S.C. §1738A, and by Oklahoma's Uniform Interstate Family Support Act, 43 O.S. §601-101 et seq. Under said acts, Oklahoma and this Court has jurisdiction to hear and determine all issues pertaining to the custody, visitation, and support of the minor children.
10. Further, it is in the best interest of the parties' minor children that this Court assume custody, visitation, and support jurisdiction under said acts because the children and these parties each have significant connections with this state and there is available in this state substantial evidence concerning the children's present and future care, protection, training, and personal relationships. No other state has child custody, visitation, and/or support jurisdiction. Each such category of jurisdiction should be exercised herein.
11. No person other than the parties hereto has or claims to have any custody or visitation rights concerning the parties' children or any of them. Neither the Oklahoma's Indian Child Welfare Act, 10 O.S. §40.1 et seq., nor the federal Indian Child Welfare Act, 25 U.S.C. §1901 et seq., apply to this proceeding. Other than this action, no other action has been filed in this or any other state in which the custody, visitation, or support of the minor children has been at issue and Petitioner has not participated in any such other litigation as a party, witness, or in any other capacity.
12. It is in the best interest of the mental, physical, and moral welfare of the minor children that their custody be awarded to the parties

Sample Petition for Divorce (Continued)

jointly in accordance with a joint custody plan to be adopted herein which makes provision for the physical custody, decision making, support, and visitation of the minor children as required by law and pursuant to the agreement of the parties. Respondent should receive standard visitation with the minor children.

13. For purposes of computing child support under the Child Support Guidelines, the parties earn or should be attributed their appropriate guideline share based upon their incomes which shall be determined later.

14. Each party should be awarded and set aside all of his or her separate property and the same should not be accounted for or included in the Court's division of the parties' marital estate. All items of marital property and marital debt should be identified and valued and should be equitably divided between the parties according to law.

Wherefore, Petitioner requests that he be granted a dissolution of marriage/divorce from Respondent; that he be granted all relief above set forth; and that Petitioner be granted all other ancillary and incidental relief to which he may be entitled as is warranted by the evidence and circumstances presented.

John Doe, Petitioner
BY:

_____

Attorney for Petitioner

STATE OF OKLAHOMA   ) ss.
   COUNTY OF _____   )

   COMES NOW John Doe, Petitioner, and after being duly sworn deposes and states that he has read the foregoing Complaint, knows the contents thereof, and that the facts contained therein are true as he verily believes.

_____

John Doe, Petitioner

Appendix

Standard Minimum Noncustodial Visitation Schedule

The parties hereto shall attempt to work together to attain maximum parental contact between themselves and their minor children. The following visitation schedule is considered by the Court as a guide for minimum contact between the parent and children. The custodial parent shall not use this guide as determining maximum contact between the noncustodial parent and the children, but rather as a guide to the Court's minimum expectations. Evening meals with the children with the noncustodial parent during the week along with phone calls during the week are strongly encouraged and recommended, as are additional periods of visitation during periods of school vacation. Failure to comply with the provisions of this minimum visitation schedule may result in a modification of custody and/or a change in visitation privileges.

The noncustodial parent shall be entitled to visitation with the minor children, named as follows:

Janet Lynn Doe, DOB: May 19, 1994; and Robert Paul Doe, DOB: December 12, 1996

Such visitation shall be at a minimum as follows:

1. **ALTERNATING WEEKENDS**

   a. Every other weekend beginning at 6:00 P.M. on Friday through 6:00 P.M. Sunday, commencing with the weekend of _____, 20__.

   b. It will be the responsibility of the noncustodial parent to pick up and deliver the children for the alternating weekend visitation periods.

2. **HOLIDAY VISITATION**

   a. *Easter Weekend.* The children shall spend Easter weekend (from Friday at 6:00 P.M. until Sunday at 6:00 P.M.) with Father during even-numbered years and with Mother during odd-numbered years.

   b. *Spring Break.* The children shall reside with each parent during one-half of Spring Break, with the transfer to occur on Wednesday evening at 6:00 P.M. The parent normally having the children during the first weekend of Spring Break shall continue to have the children until the Wednesday transfer.

   c. *Mother's Day.* The children shall spend Mother's Day (from 9:00 A.M. until 8:00 P.M.) with the children's mother.

   d. *Memorial Day.* The children shall spend the Memorial Day weekend (from Friday at 6:00 P.M. until Monday at 6:00 P.M.) with

Standard Minimum Noncustodial Visitation Schedule
(Continued)

Mother during even-numbered years and with Father during odd-numbered years.

e. ***Father's Day.*** The children shall spend Father's Day (from 9:00 A.M. until 8:00 P.M. with the children's father.

f. ***Fourth of July.*** The children shall spend the Fourth of July holiday (from 6:00 P.M. on July 3rd until 9:00 A.M. on July 5th) with Father during even-numbered years and with Mother during odd-numbered years.

g. ***Labor Day.*** The children shall spend the Labor Day weekend (from Friday at 6:00 P.M. until Monday at 6:00 P.M.) with Mother during even-numbered years and with Father during odd-numbered years.

h. ***Fall Break.*** The children shall spend Fall Break, if any, from Wednesday at 6:00 P.M. to Sunday at 5:00 P.M. with Father during odd-numbered years and with Mother during even-numbered years.

i. ***Halloween.*** The children shall spend the Halloween evening (a minimum of three hours) with Father during even-numbered years and with Mother during odd-numbered years.

j. ***Thanksgiving.*** The children shall spend Thanksgiving holiday (from Wednesday evening at 6:00 P.M. until Friday evening at 6:00 P.M.) with Mother during even-numbered years and with Father during odd-numbered years.

k. ***Pre-Christmas Period.*** The children shall spend the pre-Christmas period (from 6:00 P.M. on the day school is dismissed for vacation until 10:00 P.M. on Christmas Eve, December 24th) with Father during even-numbered years and with Mother during odd-numbered years.

l. ***Christmas Period.*** The children shall spend the Christmas period (from 10:00 P.M. on December 24th until 6:00 P.M. on December 30th) with Mother during even-numbered years and Father during odd-numbered years.

m. ***New Year's Eve and New Year's Day.*** The children shall spend from December 30th at 6:00 P.M. until 6:00 P.M. on the evening before school resumes with Father during even-numbered years and with Mother during odd-numbered years.

n. ***Holiday Transportation.*** With the exception of weekend visitation, the custodial parent is to be responsible for transportation of the children for drop-off and pickup at the home of the

Standard Minimum Noncustodial Visitation Schedule
(Continued)

noncustodial parent during the holiday visitation periods provided in this order.

3. **ADDITIONAL VISITATION PERIODS**

   a. *One Evening Per Week.* Depending upon the ages of the children and their respective school activities, the noncustodial parent may further have at least one evening per week with the children as agreed by the parties from 6:00 P.M. until 9:00 P.M. The evening will be determined by the parties each Sunday, and, if the parties cannot agree as to which evening will be utilized, then the evening will be on Thursday.

   b. *Father's Birthday.* The children shall spend the evening of Father's birthday (a minimum of three hours) with Father.

   c. *Mother's Birthday.* The children shall spend the evening of Mother's birthday (a minimum of three hours) with Mother.

4. **SUMMER VISITATION**

   a. *June Visitation.* The noncustodial parent shall further have two (2) weeks in June with the children, with the commencement of each period being determined by agreement of the parties no later than April 30th each year. If the parties cannot agree as to what weeks will be utilized, the June summer visitation will commence at 6:00 P.M. on the 1st Sunday in June through 6:00 P.M. the third Sunday in June, subject to the alternating weekend visitation by the custodial parent.

   b. *July Visitation.* The noncustodial parent shall further have two (2) weeks in July with the children, with the commencement of each period being determined by agreement of the parties no later than April 30th each year. If the parties cannot agree as to what weeks will be utilized, the July summer visitation will commence at 6:00 P.M. on the 1st Sunday in July through 6:00 P.M. the third Sunday in July, subject to the alternating weekend visitation by the custodial parent.

   c. *Two-Week Increments.* It is the intent of this order for the parties to each be allowed to make summer plans with the children for up to a duration of two (2) weeks for each visitation period. If the parties are unable to agree to such a plan, the weeks shall alternate as indicated for June and July visitation as indicated above.

5. **RULES REGARDING VISITATION**

   a. *School Calendar.* The school calendar of the school district in which the children reside(s) shall be the governing calendar to be

Standard Minimum Noncustodial Visitation Schedule
(Continued)

used to determine holidays that relate to a school calendar, even if the children is/are not yet school age.

b. ***Holidays vs. Regular Visitation.*** Holidays and special occasions shall supersede regular custody and visitation rights, and regular custody and visitation rights "lost" to holidays and special occasions shall not be "made up."

6. **OTHER PROVISIONS**

a. ***Toys and Clothes.*** Toys and clothes belonging to children should travel freely between households and shall be returned with the child in a clean and orderly manner. Children shall be allowed to feel free to take the toys and clothes they want to take with them and not restricted by which parent purchased the item.

b. ***Telephone Visitation.*** In addition to the minimum contacts indicated herein, liberal telephone communications between the noncustodial parent and children are encouraged. Unless otherwise agreed upon by the parents, "liberal telephone communications" is defined as two (2) times per week between Monday and Friday and one (1) time per weekend. If a parent uses an answering machine, messages left for the children should be returned within 24 hours. Parents should agree on a specified time for calls to the children so that the children will be made available. Telephone communications are also encouraged between the children and the custodial parent during noncustodial parent visitation.

c. ***Deviations.*** Parents are allowed to deviate from this schedule by mutual agreement with consideration at all times as to the best interest of the children.

d. ***Special Considerations.*** Special consideration should be given to each parent to make the children available to attend family functions, including funerals, weddings, family reunions, religious holidays, important ceremonies, and other significant events in the life of the children or in the life of either parent which may inadvertently conflict with this visitation schedule.

e. ***Minimum Visitation.*** It is important to be aware that this Minimum Standard Visitation Schedule is for the purpose of providing assured minimum amounts of visitation between noncustodial parent and children. Visitation should exceed the number of occasions set out within this Schedule.

Standard Minimum Noncustodial Visitation Schedule
(Continued)

f.   ***Child-Support Calculations.*** For the purposes of determining child support, the Court has determined that the visitation overnights pursuant to this Minimum Standard Visitation Schedule totals ninety (90) overnights. That number of overnights shall be utilized in any child-support guideline calculations.

This Minimum Standard Visitation Schedule is hereby approved by the Court, and is made a part of the attached Decree of Divorce and Dissolution of Marriage by reference as set forth therein, and IT IS SO ORDERED BY THIS COURT.

WITNESS MY HAND THIS _____ day of _____, 20__.

_____
JUDGE OF THE DISTRICT COURT

Resources

Annual Credit Report Request Service
P.O. Box 105283
Atlanta, GA 30348-5283
(877) 322–8228
www.annualcreditreport.com

This website offers a centralized service for consumers to request annual credit reports. It was created by the three nationwide consumer credit reporting companies: Equifax, Experian, and Trans Union. AnnualCreditReport.com processes requests for free credit file disclosures (commonly called credit reports). Under the *Fair and Accurate Credit Transactions Act (FACT Act),* consumers can request and obtain a free credit report once every twelve months from each of the three nationwide consumer credit reporting companies. AnnualCreditReport.com offers consumers a fast and convenient way to request, view, and print their credit reports in a secure Internet environment. It also provides options to request reports by telephone and by mail.

Internal Revenue Service (IRS)
www.irs.gov
Phone: (800) 829-1040 tax assistance for individual tax questions or (800) 829-4933 for business tax questions.

The IRS website allows you to search for any keyword, review publications, and information on tax questions, or submit a question via e-mail or phone to an IRS representative.

Legal Aid Services of Oklahoma, Inc.
LASO Administration
2915 North Classen Boulevard, Suite 500
Oklahoma City, OK 73106
Phone: (405) 557-0020
Toll-free: (800) 421-1641
Fax: (405) 524-1257
www.legalaidok.org

Oklahoma City University School of Law
800 North Harvey
Oklahoma City, OK 73102
Phone: (405) 208-5337
http://law.okcu.edu

Oklahoma Coalition Against
Domestic Violence and Sexual Assault
3815 North Santa Fe
Oklahoma City, OK 73118
Phone: (405) 524-0700
Fax: (405) 524-0711
http://ocadvsa.org

Oklahoma Department of Human Services
Child Support Services
P.O. Box 248822
Oklahoma City, OK 73124
Phone: Oklahoma City (405) 522-2273, Tulsa (918) 295-3500
Toll-free: (800) 522-2922
www.okdhs.org/services/ocss/Pages/default.aspx

Social Security Administration
Office of Public Inquiries
Windsor Park Building
6401 Security Boulevard
Baltimore, MD 21235
Phone: (800) 772-1213
www.ssa.gov
The website enables users to search for a question or word, submit questions via e-mail, or review recent publications.

The University of Tulsa College of Law
Boesche Legal Clinic
407 South Florence Avenue
Tulsa, OK 74104
Phone: (918) 631-5799
Toll-free: (800) 438-5909
https://law.utulsa.edu

Glossary

Alimony: Court-ordered spousal support payments from one party to another, often to enable the recipient spouse to become economically independent.

Allegation: A statement that one party claims is true.

Appeal: The process by which a higher court reviews the decision of a lower court. In Oklahoma family law cases, a person will first file an appeal with the Oklahoma Court of Appeals. After that appeal is decided there may be a further appeal to the Oklahoma Supreme Court.

Application to modify: A party's written request to the court to change a prior order regarding custody, child support, alimony, or any other order that the court may change by law.

Child support: Financial support for a child paid by the noncustodial parent to the custodial parent.

Contempt of court: The willful and intentional failure of a party to comply with a court order, judgment, or decree. Contempt may be punishable by a fine or jail.

Contested case: Any case in which the parties cannot reach an agreement. A contested case will result in a trial to have the judge decide disputed issues.

Court order: A court-issued document setting forth the judge's orders. An order can be issued based upon the parties' agreement or the judge's decision. An order may require the parties to perform certain acts or set forth their rights and responsibilities. An order is put in writing, signed by the judge, and filed with the court.

Court order acceptable for processing (COAP): A type of court order that provides for payment of civil service retirement to a former spouse.

Cross-examination: The questioning of a witness by the opposing counsel during trial or at a deposition.

Custody: The legal right and responsibility awarded by a court for the possession, care of, and decision making for a minor child.

Decree of dissolution: A final court order dissolving the marriage, dividing property and debts, ordering support, and entering other orders regarding finances and the minor children.

Deposition: A witness's testimony taken out of court, under oath, and in the presence of lawyers and a court reporter. If a person gives a different testimony at the time of trial, he or she can be impeached with the deposition testimony; that is, statements made at a deposition can be used to show untruthfulness if a different answer is given at trial.

Direct examination: The initial questioning of a witness in court by the lawyer who called him or her to the stand.

Discovery: A process used by attorneys to discover information from the opposing party for the purpose of fully assessing a case for settlement or trial. Types of discovery include interrogatories, requests for production of documents, and requests for admissions.

Dissolution: The act of terminating or dissolving a marriage.

Equitable distribution of property: The method by which real and personal property and debts are divided in a divorce. Given all economic circumstances of the parties, Oklahoma law requires that marital property and debts be divided in a fair and reasonable manner.

Ex parte: Usually in reference to a motion, the term used to describe an appearance of only one party before the judge, without the other party being present. For example, an *ex parte* emergency custody order may be granted if there are serious allegations of harm.

Guardian *ad litem* (GAL): A lawyer or mental health professional appointed by the court to conduct an investigation regarding the children's best interest.

Hearing: Any proceeding before the court for the purpose of resolving disputed issues between the parties through presentation of testimony, affidavits, exhibits, or argument.

Glossary

Hold-harmless clause: A term in a court order that requires one party to assume responsibility for a debt and to protect the other spouse from any loss or expense in connection with it, as in "to hold harmless from liability."

Interrogatories: Written questions sent from one party to the other that are used to obtain facts or opinions related to the divorce.

Joint custody: The shared right and responsibility of both parents awarded by the court for custody, care, and decision making for children.

Mediation: A process by which a neutral third party facilitates negotiations between the parties on a wide range of issues.

Motion: A written application to the court for relief, such as temporary child support, custody, or restraining orders.

No-fault divorce: The type of divorce in Oklahoma in which the court does not require evidence of marital misconduct. This means that abandonment, cruelty, and adultery are neither relevant nor required to be proven for the purposes of granting the divorce.

Notice of hearing: A written statement sent to the opposing lawyer or spouse listing the date and place of a hearing and the nature of the matters that will be heard by the court. In Oklahoma, one party is required to give the other party reasonable notice of any court hearing.

Party: The person in a legal action whose rights or interests will be affected by the divorce. For example, in a divorce the parties include the wife and husband.

Pending: During the case. For example, the judge may award you temporary support while your case is pending.

Petition: The legal document that starts the divorce and tells the court what you are requesting.

Petitioner: The person who files the petition initiating a divorce.

Pleadings: Documents filed with the court seeking a court order.

Qualified domestic relations order (QDRO): A type of court order that provides for direct payment from a retirement account to a former spouse.

Qualified medical support order (QMSO): A type of court order that provides a former spouse certain rights regarding medical insurance and information.

Request for production of documents: A written request for documents sent from one party to the other during the discovery process.

Respondent: The spouse who was served with the petition. In Oklahoma they were formerly called the *defendant.*

Response: A written response to the petition for divorce. It serves to admit or deny the allegations in the petition and may also make claims against the opposing party. This is sometimes called a responsive pleading or an answer. A response should be filed within twenty days of either (a) the petition being served by the process server or (b) the defendant's voluntary appearance being filed with the court.

Sequester: To order prospective witnesses out of the courtroom until they have concluded giving their testimony.

Setoff: A debt or financial obligation of one spouse that is deducted from the debt or financial obligation of the other spouse.

Settlement: The agreed resolution of disputed issues.

Show-cause hearing: A hearing that typically occurs within ten days of some type of emergency relief being requested whether it is in child custody or a protective order hearing.

Stipulation: An agreement reached between parties or an agreement by their attorneys.

Subpoena: A document delivered to a person or witness that requires him or her to appear in court, appear for a deposition, or produce documents. Failure to comply could result in punishment by the court. A subpoena requesting documents is called a *subpoena duces tecum.*

Temporary restraining order: An order of the court prohibiting a party from certain behavior. For example, a temporary restraining order goes into effect once the respondent is served with the automatic temporary injunction.

Trial: A formal court hearing in which the judge will decide disputed issues raised by the parties' pleadings.

Under advisement: A term used to describe the status of a case, usually after a court hearing on a motion or a trial, when the judge has not yet made a decision.

Index

Index

credit cards, 129-131
debt accrual during divorce process and, 131
hold-harmless clause and, 132
house payments, 129-130
mortgage refinancing and, 132-133
pre-marriage debt and, 131-132
student loans, 131debt accrual during decree of dissolution of divorce, 18
decree, 33
default divorce, 8
defendant, 10
denial, 28
Department of Human Services (DHS), 89, 96, 99, 102
divorce process, 131
dependents, claiming of, 138-139
deponent, 57
deposition
defined, 25-26, 52, 54
fear of, 25
impeaching for lying during, 55, 57
judge, reading of, 55
necessity of, 60
non-responsive witnesses during, 58
perjury during, 57
preparing for, 56
purpose of, 54-55
questions asked during, 56-58
suggestions for successful, 58-60
truthfulness during, 55
of all witnesses, 60
depression about divorce, 23-24
destroying assets, 121
discovery, 17, 33, 51-53, *see also* discovery process
discovery process, 51-60, *see*

also discovery; deposition
attorney, role in, 34-35
child custody during, 78, 81
deadlines for, 53
length of time for, 52
subpoenas during, 54
dismissing divorce, 24-25
Disneyland parent, 23
dissolution of marriage, 32
division of assets proposal, 112
divorce, *see also* filing for divorce; divorce process; granting divorce; fees for divorce
acceptance of, 28
agreement to, 3
amicable, 17, 36
children, talking about, 22
counseling during, 24
depression about, 23-24
dismissing, 24-25
emotional passages experienced during, 28
finality of, 18-19
grounds for, 2-3
length of time for, 18
petition for, 9, 155-157
sadness about, 24-25
shame about, 25
spouse's agreement to, 3
waiting period for, 9
divorce issues checklist, 15-17
divorce petition, 9, 12
divorce process, 1-19, *see also* divorce
responsibilities during, 14-15
steps in, 2, 4-7
stress during, coping with, 20-28
understanding, 1-19
documents, *see also* discovery process
for negotiations, 17
obtaining copies of, 48-49

Index

Index

Index

About the Author

Mark Antinoro, J.D., is an attorney in private practice and is founder of the Antinoro Law Firm in Pryor, Oklahoma. He has practiced law for two decades. He earned his baccalaureate degree from Albertus Magnus College in New Haven, Connecticut. He earned his Juris Doctor from University of Tulsa College of Law. Mr. Antinoro is an AV-rated attorney who specializes in family law. He has been named a Rising Star by Super Lawyers. Mr. Antinoro was selected by his fellow attorneys to represent seventeen counties in northeastern Oklahoma on the Oklahoma Judicial Nominating Commission. He served for six years on the Oklahoma Judicial Nominating Commission and at the time he was the youngest elected chairman in its history. Mr. Antinoro is a member of the Family Law Section of the Oklahoma Bar Association.

Mr. Antinoro is also a certified mediator. He is widely known in northeastern Oklahoma for his ability to settle contested custody and divorce matters

Mark lives in Owasso, Oklahoma, with his wife, Svetlana, and their son, Ashton. He may be contacted by telephone at (918) 825-3700 or at his website: **www.antinorolaw.com.**

Divorce Titles from Addicus Books

Visit our online catalog at www.AddicusBooks.com

Divorce in Alabama: The Legal Process, Your Rights, and What to Expect $21.95

Divorce in Arizona: The Legal Process, Your Rights, and What to Expect. $21.95

Divorce in California: The Legal Process, Your Rights, and What to Expect $21.95

Divorce in Connecticut: The Legal Process, Your Rights, and What to Expect $21.95

Divorce in Florida: The Legal Process, Your Rights, and What to Expect $21.95

Divorce in Georgia: Simple Answers to Your Legal Questions $21.95

Divorce in Hawaii: The Legal Process, Your Rights, and What to Expect $21.95

Divorce in Illinois: The Legal Process, Your Rights, and What to Expect $21.95

Divorce in Kansas: The Legal Process, Your Rights, and What to Expect $21.95

Divorce in Louisiana: The Legal Process, Your Rights, and What to Expect $21.95

Divorce in Maine: The Legal Process, Your Rights, and What to Expect $21.95

Divorce in Maryland: The Legal Process, Your Rights, and What to Expect $21.95

Divorce in Michigan: The Legal Process, Your Rights, and What to Expect. $21.95

Divorce in Mississippi: The Legal Process, Your Rights, and What to Expect. $21.95

A Guide to Divorce in Missouri: Simple Answers to Complex Questions $21.95

Divorce in Nebraska: The Legal Process, Your Rights, and What to Expect—2nd Edition $21.95

Divorce in Nevada: The Legal Process, Your Rights, and What to Expect. $21.95

Divorce in New Jersey: The Legal Process, Your Rights, and What to Expect $21.95

Divorce in New York: The Legal Process, Your Rights, and What to Expect $21.95

Divorce in North Carolina: Answers to Your Legal Questions. $21.95

Divorce in Oklahoma: The Legal Process, Your Rights, and What to Expect $21.95

Divorce in Tennessee: The Legal Process, Your Rights, and What to Expect $21.95

Divorce in Virginia: The Legal Process, Your Rights, and What to Expect $21.95

Divorce in Washington: The Legal Process, Your Rights, and What to Expect $21.95

Divorce in West Virginia: The Legal Process, Your Rights, and What to Expect $21.95

Divorce in Wisconsin: The Legal Process, Your Rights, and What to Expect $21.95

Daily Meditations for Healing from Divorce: Discovering the New You. $21.95

To Order Books:

Visit us online at: www.AddicusBooks.com

Call toll free: (800) 888-4741

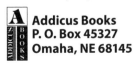

Addicus Books
P. O. Box 45327
Omaha, NE 68145

To order books from Addicus Books:

Please send:

_____copies of_____
(Title of book)
at \$ _____each   TOTAL _____
NE residents add 5% sales tax   _____

Add Shipping/Handling
    \$6.75 for first book
    \$1.10 for each additional book _____

TOTAL ENCLOSED   _____

Name _____
Address _____
City _____State_____Zip _____

☐ Visa   ☐ Mastercard   ☐ AMEX   ☐ Discover
Credit card number _____
Expiration date _____
Three digit CVV number on back of card _____

Order by credit card or personal check.

To Order Books:
Visit us online at: www.AddicusBooks.com
Call toll free: (800) 888-4741

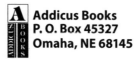

Addicus Books
P. O. Box 45327
Omaha, NE 68145